INTRODUCING BOOKS TO
CHILDREN

INTRODUCING BOOKS
TO CHILDREN

by

Aidan Chambers

HEINEMANN EDUCATIONAL BOOKS
LONDON

Heinemann Educational Books Ltd
LONDON EDINBURGH MELBOURNE AUCKLAND TORONTO
SINGAPORE HONG KONG KUALA LUMPUR
IBADAN JOHANNESBURG NAIROBI
LUSAKA NEW DELHI

ISBN 0 435 80260 7 (cased)
ISBN 0 435 80261 5 (paperback)

Published by
Heinemann Educational Books Ltd
48 Charles Street, London W1X 8AH
Printed in Great Britain by
Butler & Tanner Ltd, Frome and London

Contents

Preface

This book has been written for teachers, particularly student-teachers and beginners in the profession, and for anyone who is concerned about how to help children become avid, willing, enthusiastic readers. It is an attempt to take a straightforward and practical look at ideas, methods, varying approaches which bring books and young people into contact.

Though I have touched briefly here and there on the teaching of literature – close study of prescribed texts during curricula work in school – I have deliberately avoided extensive consideration of this aspect of the subject. It seems to me that if such directed study is to have any permanent value, children must first be avid, unreluctant readers. And so I have concentrated my attention on what can be done to get them this far. Besides, teaching literature is a specialist work; as George Sampson remarked years ago, 'The plain fact is that every teacher cannot deal with literature and we must not expect every teacher to deal with it.' But every teacher can and should play a part in encouraging children to read voraciously. That is what this book is primarily about. As a result, there remains an unresolved tension. There are moments in the pages that follow when I seem to contradict myself. At one moment I say – putting it crudely now – that it doesn't matter what children read so long as they read widely. At another moment I say discrimination is all important. How to resolve this paradox (for it isn't actually a contradiction at all)? That question needs another whole book to itself, and so, in this one, must remain unexplored. There are plenty of hints, however, to indicate the directions I would take.

The first three chapters are concerned with why literary reading above all is important to everyone, and sketch in the general background against which the next seven chapters of practical explorations must be set. As no book is ever exhaustive (and this one, intended for the novice rather than the experienced practitioner, is hardly more than a preliminary canter over the terrain), my deep hope is that many readers will want to follow up the sources of further explication and information which I have found useful and which are cited after each chapter, as well as the expanded lists of aids and references that make up the concluding bibliography. Finally, some articles by other writers that seem to add significantly to points made in the body of the text but which it would have been inconvenient to quote at length are brought together in a hotch-potch collection of appendices.

A few things I would ask be kept in mind throughout. A slight matter first: these days it is necessary to assure some people that when one uses 'he' as a pronoun in place of 'the child' so beloved of all who utter on educational themes, one of course means to include girls as well as boys. No dominance or indeed preference (in this context at least) is either intended or implied. I simply refuse to depersonalize 'the child' by turning him-or-her into it. Rather more serious and difficult is the problem of ages and stages: the ages when children might best be introduced to particular books by particular methods, and the stages of the educational system – pre-school, infant, primary, middle-school, secondary, etc. – that can best make use of this or that approach. Much of what I have said applies to all ages and stages, but nevertheless I have tried not to tie down my remarks too specifically in this regard. Teaching is an art, not a science, and those who practise it will rightly prefer to decide for themselves which of my suggestions have anything to offer the children for whom they work. My only plea is for a whole view to be taken. For the sake of coherence and order the text is marshalled into chapters, each of which treats of one broad issue. But none of them is, in fact, a separate entity: they interweave, support each other, are never enough on their own as a basis for a complete teaching programme. We have suffered for too long from a single approach to the encouragement of reading. Rich diversity is more likely to succeed.

This book grew out of many discussions with other teachers. I offer it in the same spirit that informed those encounters: a desire to share what we had learned, and to push out the boundaries of our skill and understanding.

A.C.

Amberley, June 1973

Acknowledgements

Copyright details are given in the main text, but to the owners of quoted passages I here offer my thanks for permission to use their words. Many children, teachers and friends have helped me, tangibly and intangibly, in the writing of this book. To all of them I am grateful, and particularly I owe a debt of gratitude to: Janet Hill, a children's librarian of generous sympathies and inexhaustible energy who has supplied me with encouragement as well as information; Alan Tucker, a bookseller with the rare attribute of knowing what is inside a book as well as what it costs, and a friend who has charged me with ideas; Don Carlyon, Trevor Dickenson and Jim Osborn, three inspired teachers whose work with children and books has shown me what can be achieved. Last of all, because she is first of all, my thanks to Nancy, my wife.

Note: Figures expressed thus (1) indicate references to be found at the end of the relevant chapter.

ONE

Why bother?

In a jumble of old papers I recently came across the photograph of a young man striding through a classroom door, a pile of books under his arm and an eager look in his eyes. From the way his left shoulder is tipped forward, from the set of his head and the length of his stride, one gets the feeling that he is a fully clothed sprinter just leaving the starting blocks. The young man is, of course, myself snapped fifteen years or so ago by a cheeky thirteen-year-old during the first few months of my first teaching job. When I see that photograph now I smile, but the young man doesn't seem to have any connection with myself.

He does, however, remind me of the way I went about my business in those early days of my teaching career; and I mention him here because his experiences parallel, I think, those of many young teachers in their first few months at work. I remember, to begin with, that the eager young man enjoyed himself greatly; and, for the most part, so did the boys he taught. But I now know he had not a clue about what he was doing. He had vague ideas – which, at the time, he thought very clear ideas – and his teacher training had been helpful, stimulating even, and informative enough; but when he got into the classroom he quickly discovered that neither his ideas nor his training were much help when it actually came to doing a full day's work every school day, every school week for a school year. In college, mostly for the benefit of supervisory lecturers, he had given set-piece lessons prepared in meticulous detail but hardly at all linked to the context of life lived by the children he taught during his stint of teaching practice. Things may be better now in the preparation of teachers for their profession; but some of the problems I'm trying to get at remain, and always will remain, because of the nature of that curious occupation.

Faith and arrogance got that eager young man through his first full-time months. The faith was pretty blind and the arrogance, luckily, borne with uncomplaining good humour by the rest of his colleagues. From the beginning he spent a lot of time and energy trying to get his pupils to read. The books included not only texts prescribed by the syllabus, texts he sometimes loathed almost as much as the children they were inflicted upon loathed them, but also a wide selection of books chosen mostly because he had liked them himself in adolescence, or because he felt his pupils ought at least to have tasted them. Both his selection and his methods of introducing the books were guided more by intuition than thoughtful planning. It was all a somewhat hit-and-miss affair; if there was a philosophy underlying what he did, it was simplistic. Reading books, he believed, was important (though he could not have said precisely why) and so it was his job as an English teacher to encourage his pupils to read. The best way to do that was to let his own genuine enthusiasm show, and by energy, amusement, pure force of personality, to draw his classes into enjoying books first of all with him and then on their own.

To some extent this worked. Haphazardly perhaps, but in a cheerful atmosphere that, though he did not realize it then, glossed over the inadequacies of his approach. It is very easy for a teacher to think he is succeeding just because his pupils are lively and laughing. Only as his experience accumulated did this young man see that what he did was littered as much, if not more, with failure as with success of a lasting kind. Then he came to a stop and asked himself what he was doing and why.

At first, analysing the way he went about his work eroded his confidence, threw him off balance, dimmed some of the energetic sparkle. No one likes to admit, to himself least of all, that he has been wrong, or, at best, inadequate and cack-handed. But that pain passed with the understanding that what one thinks and the way one thinks profoundly influence what one does and the way one does it. Intuition is all very well, a few bright ideas are useful, an entertaining approach and a charming personality put to work with energy are strong assets. But they are all shifting sands to build on. What one needs above all is a coherent set of attitudes, a conscious understanding of the function and value of what one is doing and teaching.

I begin with this embarrassing third person autobiographical note not because I fancy it elevates me (I don't; in fact, I am shame-faced when I think of the time it took that raw young man to realize the error of his ways) but because I think it parallels the experience of many young teachers, and also because it explains why I attach so much importance to beginning a basically practical book with such a question as 'Why bother?' Why bother so much about children's reading? Why bother about the methods of introducing books to children? We need answers to this double-edged question because, unless we are clear about the answers, we are likely to make a number of gross mistakes in trying to bring children and books together in a tensile and lasting connection. And to make sure why we believe it important to bring children up as willing, avid, responsive readers of literature we have to go back a step further still and sort out why literature is important to ourselves. In taking this step back we lay bare our own attitudes to books and reading and the place they hold in our lives – attitudes which will inevitably colour whatever methods we employ with children, and which are influential in more ways than that they simply affect our teaching methods. Of all the forces at work on children, attracting them to or repelling them from the printed word, and there are many, the attitude of adults they meet frequently in their daily lives, which means parents and teachers more than any others, wields an effect surpassed only by the attitude of children's intimate peers. The stance these adults take up is assumed by children (whether consciously or not doesn't matter) to be the stance taken up by society as a whole. And the value society places on books matters a lot. Reading is hard work, much harder work than experienced adult readers remember, for to them the hard work has become a pleasure, part of the thing they enjoy in reading, as a sportsman enjoys the physical effort involved in playing his game. If a child detects no very strong response between adults and books, especially during the early stages of learning to read for himself, then he feels no compelling impetus to develop his own reading skill beyond a certain very minimal level, the level of reading signs and newspapers and magazines and the need to gather information in work or leisure.

This is why there is such a marked relationship between children who quickly and permanently become avid readers and a home-and-school environment where books are thought important, are frequently used, often discussed, and everywhere in evidence. I say 'home-and-school' deliberately. For too long we imagined that schools could do the job on their own, and indeed they have achieved great things. But ultimately we have to acknowledge that the best and most lasting success comes only when the home environment is right-minded too. We have, in fact, at last begun to recognize that any child who comes to school at five without certain kinds of literary experience is a deprived child in whose growth there are deficiencies already difficult to make good.

(This home-and-school setting, by the way, is not necessarily simply to do with class, with social background, as some people tend to suggest. There are homes-and-schools in financially poor areas where books come in for the same everyday, pleasurable attention as they do in some more affluent places; and equally there are better-off settings where the attitude to books is so poverty-stricken that the children are virtually illiterate: they can decipher words on a page with the best of them, but they rarely read in the considered sense of that much abused word. Readers are not made by money and class, thank goodness, or there would be little hope for most of us.)

What is there, then, to be so valued in literature that we attach the central, over-riding importance to it that we do? It is a tricky question, complicated and slithery; and the opening statements have rarely been better put than by Richard Hoggart in the first paragraph of a seminal essay, 'Why I Value Literature':

> I value literature because of the way – the peculiar way – in which it explores, re-creates and seeks for the meanings in human experience; because it explores the diversity, complexity and strangeness of that experience (of individual men or of men in groups or of men in relation to the natural world); because it re-creates the texture of that experience; and because it pursues its explorations with disinterested passion (not wooing nor apologizing nor bullying). I value literature because in it men look at life with all the vulnerability, honesty, and penetration they can command . . . and dramatize their insights by means of a unique relationship with language and form. (1. p. 11)

Professor Hoggart's own teasing out of that compact statement occupies the rest of his short essay, essential reading on this theme to which I owe a debt I gladly acknowledge. Indeed the full text is so useful in clearing the general ground on which the rest of this chapter rests that I have reprinted the whole of it as Appendix 1 and hope that it will be studied by readers at this point.

For my own purpose I need now to expand on this general statement in directions pertinent to the theme of children and literature. But before setting out on that track, I had better clear up what I mean by literature, a word that has come to mean many things. There is, for example, the literature dispensed by travel agents to people who inquire about holidays, and the literature prescribed by GCE examination boards as being suitable for boys and girls of sixteen to answer questions about; or there is literature in the collective, bibliographic sense, meaning all that has been written on any given topic no matter what its nature or purpose. Much that follows in this book could apply equally to any kind of reading matter brought before children. But as I am here principally using the word I mean 'any kind of composition in prose or verse which has for its purpose not the communication of fact but the telling of a story (either wholly invented or given new life through invention) or the giving of pleasure through some use of the inventive imagination in the employment'.*

This is not, of course, a critical definition, but simply an attempt to mark out some limits – limits which would enclose *Beano* as well

---

* I have borrowed this useful clarification from David Daiches' *Critical Approaches to Literature* (Longman). Professor Daiches continues with the following words which may be of further help: 'There is, oddly enough, no single word in English that corresponds to the Greek *poesis* or the German *Dichtung*, terms which refer to products of the literary imagination and do not include, as the term *literature* does, anything at all that is written. The term *poetry* as used by some earlier writers – by Sir Philip Sidney, for example, in his *Apologie for Poetrie* – has the wider meaning of *poesis* or *Dichtung*, but it has since narrowed in meaning, just as *literature* has become too wide.'

as *Where the Wild Things Are*, Enid Blyton as well as Mark Twain, street songs and rhymes as well as Wordsworth's *Prelude*, graffiti as well as *Ulysses*. Criticism will come later; all that need be said here is that quite obviously works of literature admitted by such a delineation will differ in the extent to which they match up to Professor Hoggart's statement of value. But the outcome of critical assessments of specific books is not relevant at this point in the discussion; all I wish to do is to examine the value of literature as a whole.

Children, language and literature

Hoggart's key phrase, 'explores, re-creates and seeks for meanings', brings us at once into an understanding of the value of literature for children. You would have to go a long way to find a better description of the essential vocation of childhood than that it is a time when people explore, re-create and seek for meanings in human experience with a greater intensity than at any other period in their lives. Children are occupied thus every day in their natural, instinctive play. Sound educational practice formalizes and directs play, trying to make the child aware of what he discovers at a speed and to a degree that, without adult aid – without 'education' – would take much longer to come by, even if the same degree of awareness was ever reached at all. Clearly, any form of human expression which has at its heart this same purpose, and helps people to continue in it beyond their childhood years, must be brought into the centre not only of school education but of the child's life outside school.

Literature, if we accept what Hoggart and very many others say, has such a purpose. But it is not alone in this. Music, the manual arts, genuine scientific inquiry (as against technology, which is not truth-seeking) all in one way and another explore and seek for meanings. What these others do not share between them or with literature is literature's particular attribute, 'a unique relationship with language and form'. So the place of language needs closer examination, which will directly lead us to an examination of form.

Ranking among the daftest exercises sometimes imposed on children is the one that requires them to describe a screwdriver or a vase or the desks they sit at, or any familiar object. They are being asked to perform what C. S. Lewis called 'an eccentric *tour de force*', for language is 'the worst tool in the world for communicating knowledge of complex three dimensional shapes'. Coleridge had already noted the result of such hapless pedagogy: 'all is so dutchified by the most minute touches that the reader asks why words and not painting were used.' The stupidity of such classroom grind is usually obvious to the children forced into it, if not to their teachers. 'Imagine,' these dominies tend to begin, 'that a chap from outer space has come to earth. Describe a screwdriver to him as clearly as you can.' The space man, poor fellow, has presumably wandered up and somehow indicated that his UFO has conked out and can you help him please? In a flash, without a moment wasted on intelligent astonishment, the poor accosted mortal gives a detailed description of the instrument he apparently assumes without further investigation the stranded space man needs. Apart from all the other curious oddities in the teacher's imagined situation, the problem of language, on which the exchange rests, is not allowed to obtrude into the exercise, even if some smart-alec child raises it. Teacher forges ahead, happy in the knowledge that he is teaching his pupils how to write descriptive English. In fact, of course, all he is doing by forming the exercise in this fashion is to teach a misuse, not to say a misunderstanding, of language. This is a large and difficult question and I can hardly do more here than crudely touch it on the nerve. James Britton's invaluable book *Language and Learning*, however, makes a detailed, sensitive and clearly written examination of the subject and includes the following passage, which pin-points precisely what I'm trying to get at.

> The cutting into segments of the stream of sense experience and the recognition of similarities between segments enables us to build up a representation, let us say, of an object such as a cup. From the overlap of many experiences, focused upon as the word 'cup' is used by other people or ourselves, the basis of similarity and dissimilarity becomes more clearly defined and more objects, different from the original cup in what does not matter but alike in what does – what defines the category – are admitted to the category. The word, then, unlike the visual image I have of a cup I have seen and can recall, is a generalized representation, classifying as it represents.
>
> Taking a leap from there, it is difficult to imagine how some experiences could be classified at all were it not for the agency of language. Four-year-old children will cheerfully and confidently talk about their *holidays* – about who is on holiday and where they have gone, and about what they are going to do on their own holidays. The definition of the category, criteria by which to decide what is properly called 'a holiday' and what is not, would be a complicated task for us and certainly the four-year-old could not attempt it. And there is nothing to point to, as he might point to a cup to show he knew the meaning. The ability to operate the category has grown from the overlap of experiences of the *word in use* as applied to his own familiar experiences. (2. pbk ed. pp. 26–27)

Words are symbols; their power lies not in themselves but in what they name and stand for and all the circumstances surrounding our experience in coming to understand those symbols. Children need to reach an appreciation of this, just as they need to appreciate that words and what they stand for tend to become one in our minds, so that we have sometimes only to speak a word to witness a reaction in other people that should logically follow only if the object itself were present. As when 'Spider!' is bellowed at someone who does not exactly care for arachnids. Words are powerful, forming and motivating people's behaviour. Language, primitive minds have always believed not without some truth, is magic.

When we come to deal with our imaginings, our thoughts, emotions, past experiences in an attempt to sort them out, the power of language is not only an indispensable energy but drives deep indeed. Often, until we have forged these experiences into words we are not sure what we think, feel, know. 'How can I know what I think till I see what I say?' the poet Auden has written, echoing not only a poet's realization but a universal one. Most people can find no meaning, no order, cannot even recognize their existence until they have formed their perceptions into words or found them reflected in someone else's words. St John was only too right: in the beginning was the Word.

This is true of adults, and true even more affectively of children, who cannot yet comprehend in abstract terms. They experience so much that is new and unknown to them every day: a flood tide of sensual receptions, emotions, events, ideas, data of all kinds. Much work in education is an endless attempt to help children to learn how to articulate this confusion of experiences and so come to grips with it. Without language, the basic and demotic tool, no one would have a chance; we would go bumping round in the dark, and eventually take leave of our senses under the welter of the incomprehensible, withdrawing, as some people do, into a closed world in order to protect ourselves against the unbearable on-slaught.

Language is demotic because man needed it; he did not invent it as a way of passing the time, like a great big crossword puzzle; and the more developed and subtle it becomes, the greater its power. By it we are led to awareness, making intelligible what would otherwise be unintelligible. Language is creative, civilizing. And because this is so we recognize the importance to children of being brought up with as much control of it as possible. And more, that they understand the variety of uses it can be put to, a theme that will enter the discussion again.

In gaining that control, in reaching that understanding, we also know that above all children need a wide experience of spoken language, and that their ability to come to grips with literary uses of language depends upon this primary experience. Literature itself is built on a bedrock of speech; what we expect from literature, what we are able to take from it, and bring to it, depends crucially on what we have come to expect of speech. If our knowledge of the spoken word is restricted (and many children's knowledge is) to simple question and answer uttered in tones of only a few kinds, determined by the need to express the least of human pleasures, demands and requirements, then literary language, when it is eventually met, seems as strange as an unknown foreign language to alien ears. The link between speech and literature is of course forged early in life through story-telling and reading aloud, which prepare a child for that unique relationship with language and form he will encounter when he reads for himself.

The writer's gift is that he uses the same instrument everyone else uses every day, only he orchestrates it better. Reading therefore extends our own capacity with language; instead of struggling alone, locked in our inadequacy with words, we couple with the writer in an act of verbal creation in which communication is consummated. And so, as C. S. Lewis has noted in an extraordinarily useful little book, *An Experiment in Criticism* (3), we transcend our self without undermining our individuality. We do not merge with the writer; we simply benefit by the addition of his gift. Once aware of that possibility we do not lightly reject what literature has to offer. For unless we possess within our own being all the power of imagination we want and need, unless we are satisfied that our individual gift with language can find all the meaning and significance we look for in our sensual and imaginative perceptions and all other human experience as well, unless we have all the time, energy and ability to experience all we wish to experience, unless we believe we can do all this unaided, then we had better pay heed to literature and pay heed attentively.

Given a chance, children soon learn this and pay heed. They are happy enough to listen to stories, and go to books, once they have met them, with no apparent difficulty. The trouble is that their willingness is only superficial; it not only needs encouragement but is all too easily weakened by inculcated attitudes which stultify that willing response. What we are witnessing when we meet a child in reaction against books is not something the child was born with, but rather something imposed upon him or instilled, usually by adults. Which brings us at once face to face with the importance of our understanding the methods by which books are introduced to children.

An even stronger and more subtle cause for the rejection of literature, especially in adolescence, is that children have not been well enough taught the different ways in which language can be used, and, as a corollary, the different ways language can be read. In science the effort is to find a fixed, unchanging meaning for words; and so scientific language – and to some extent all purely factual uses of language – tries to employ words in as objective and unvarying a way as possible. When words fail to behave themselves, as they frequently do, scientists tend to invent a new language composed of tightly defined symbols to express their thoughts and discoveries. Language in literature, however, is used in such a way as to fuse disparate experiences into coherent wholes; the subjective and the objective, the personal and specific with the general and universal. Literary language is vital, shifting, fluid; it looks constantly for new structures, new combinations that strike out new meanings. It is concrete, employs images, especially metaphor, and images say several things at once. Irony and paradox bring the disparate and hitherto unconnected into relationship revealing new shades of meaning, or refreshing the worn, the tired, the clichéd.

Thus literary language is a living language, rebellious against imprisonment in the past but ever ready to feed on what has gone before. In *Little Gidding* T. S. Eliot has some lines that express what I mean not just by saying it but by demonstrating it too:

> Last season's fruit is eaten
> And the fullfed beast shall kick the empty pail.
> For last year's words belong to last year's language
> And next year's words await another voice.

This is why we quite often find that literary language deliberately explodes dictionary definitions; and by the particular way a particular author uses his words, selects and orders them, they take on a highly personal colour we call his style.

Always, the attempt in literature when it is at its best is to catch a truth of life, life in its diversity, complexity, familiar strangeness, and to re-create its very texture. And by catching it thus, like a butterfly in a net of words, an author enables himself and others to lay hold of and to contemplate experience, although the experience itself slips away beyond recall even as we live through it. In literature we lay hold of experience not in abstract, discursive terms of the kind a scientist or a philosopher might use, but by 'telling', by making in words a story, a picture. We dramatize. This power to bring an experience back to life through words is the old magic of the poets and story-tellers and playwrights. And it is one of mankind's primeval activities.

If verbal re-enactment is necessary to adults, how much more essential it must be to children, for whom it is often the only satisfactory way of handling their experience. The ability to contemplate in abstract terms is a sophisticated one, belonging to a stage of maturity which in children is only incipient.

In exercising his art the literary writer is the emanuensis of his time; through his work we are brought into direct contact not only with ourselves and our contemporaries but with the whole long line of mankind back to our primitive, elemental roots.

Not all writers by any means reach down into the depths of experience as profoundly as those we call great; some might even mislead and confuse us. But at its best this is what literature does; and without knowledge of it, even of a slight kind, we may remain uncomprehending people, vaguely sensing what we could be, both in our self and as a society, but frustrated to the point of barbaric violence because we know we are in a self-immolating prison of loneliness, unable to articulate the stirrings that boil deep within us. We need not look far to witness the acts of exasperation to which those are driven who have lost, if they ever found, the ability to articulate experience to themselves and to others; such acts happen on the streets every day.

Everyone who is a reader has his own list of books which at different times in his life opened his eyes anew. High on mine when I was fifteen and first read it was D. H. Lawrence's *Sons and Lovers*. It was like an elutriate, that book, clarifying myself to myself as well as showing me I was not alone: I suddenly realized that there were others who thought and felt as I did. I was never quite the same afterwards. A bit later in life *Pride and Prejudice* moved me quite as deeply in a different way. Here was a world and a collection of people so strange that I was spellbound with fascination, as an explorer might stand staring at a new land and an alien race. And the further I went into that foreign domain the more I began to recognize facets of behaviour, motivations, characters, which struck familiar chords. Jane Austen taught me the power of literature to open up different worlds, strange people, while at the same time showing the relationship of those worlds and people to the world and people I know and belong to.

Let me offer two other voices in summary of these aspects of the value of literature: that it is conciliatory, comforting us in our shared humanity; and that it is subversive, challenging our prejudices, and ingrained attitudes. First, here is C. S. Lewis in *An Experiment in Criticism*:

> This, so far as I can see, is the specific value or good of literature . . . it admits us to experiences other than our own. They are not, any more than our personal experiences, all equally worth having. Some, as we say, 'interest' us more than others. The causes of this interest are naturally extremely various and differ from one man to another; it may be the typical (and we say 'How true!') or the abnormal (and we say 'How strange!'); it may be the beautiful, the terrible, the awe-inspiring, the exhilarating, the pathetic, the comic, or the merely piquant. Literature gives the *entrée* to them all. (3. pp. 139–140)

And now Lionel Trilling in his Introduction to *Huckleberry Finn*, a book which was

> once barred from certain libraries and schools for its alleged sub-
> version of morality. The authorities had in mind the book's endemic
> lying, the petty thefts, the denigrations of respectability and religion,
> the bad language and the bad grammar. We smile at the excessive
> care, yet in point of fact *Huckleberry Finn* is indeed a subversive book
> – no one who reads thoughtfully the dialectic of Huck's great moral
> crisis will ever again be wholly able to accept without some question
> and some irony the assumptions of the respectable morality by which
> he lives, nor will ever again be certain that what he considers the
> clear dictates of moral reason are not merely the engrained customary
> beliefs of his time and place.*

Somehow we have to bring children to an understanding that this
is what literature is all about and what it is trying to do in the way
it puts language to work. But this understanding can only come
gradually, and only when there is first of all a groundwork of
literary experience that has entertained as well as enlightened.

Literature as action

Certainly, children come to reading for amusement; if a book does
not yield immediate pleasure they tend to lay it aside. But that is a
superficial requirement. Whether consciously or not, like adults,
they take much more from what they read than trite satisfaction.
Before one becomes a mature, avid reader, however, one has to
recognize in literature an active agent, part of the chemistry of
daily life. And there is an unfortunate implication in the way some
people talk about reading which suggests that they see it as a substitute for action, a pastime that decorates the margins of the
serious business of existence. They seem to regard literature as a
secondary, vicarious experience (if they think of it as an experience
at all), more akin to the experience of a peeping Tom, an impotent
voyeur watching healthy, active people get on with real living.

This is an important charge to counter, for it sets up an attitude
that wreaks a good deal of damage to the growth of children as
readers. That it is an attitude often taken up in unthinking ignorance does not help; and it is easier to explode in argument than it is
to eradicate in fact. Children who have already been instilled with
this attitude will ask why they should read books (they usually
mean literature rather than non-fiction, which appeals directly to
their immediate practical interests), and they want to know why
they should be bothered with lessons that attempt to introduce
them to literature.

* Lionel Trilling, Introduction to *Huckleberry Finn*, Rinehart, New York
1948, p. xiii.

Some of the apologetics which make sense to children are worth rehearsing. To start with, no one can engage 'directly' in the whole range of human experiences, not even the full range of those counted worth having. There is neither time nor opportunity in one life. But even supposing there were, it would still not be possible. How can a western-born white man, to take an extreme example, experience directly what it is like to be a black central African? Or vice versa? He can try by going to live with a black central African and getting as close to his way of existence as can be contrived. But he will soon discover that even then all the accidents of birth, up-bringing, education and social history will prevent his truly knowing the very thing he wants to know. To get really close he must make an act of imaginative projection and have communicated to him the inner realities which only the African can possibly know. One reading of a good story or poem by his African fellow may do more to make that communicative connection than months of 'direct' experience. In this respect engagement in literature is an action more effective than any other open to us.

Nor can we, to explore another avenue, directly experience what it was like to be alive in an historical time, in, say, Elizabethan England; the space-time barrier prevents it. The only way in is through the literature of the time. It is true that painting, music, architecture, and surviving 'realia' all help; but not as literature can, for literature re-creates the texture of experience.

> No other art makes us feel so much that the experience must have been just like that, that desire and will and thought would all have been caught up with those gestures, those smells, those sounds. It's not reality; it's a mirroring; but it mirrors more nearly than any other imaginative activity the *whole* sense of an experience. (1. p. 13)

Most people can elaborate this side of the argument further and children, once shown the way, will bring out examples that drive hard into their experiential desires which only literature can satisfy. What is it like to be a footballer, a nurse, a burglar, a pilot, a mother, a patient in hospital? There are a thousand and one possibilities in life which children quite as much as adults would like to experience but know they cannot by any means that are *emotionally* as well as intellectually affective, except by literature. Once this is realized, reading takes on an attraction and an importance that extends beyond pastime pleasure, a substitute for 'doing'.

But there are more telling if more complex considerations yet. Everyone is aware of the number of courses of action open to us at any one time, even allowing for hidden impulses, unconscious drives and the rest of the unwitting controls which, behavioural scientists tell us, work against ideas of freedom of choice and self-determination. Without an ability to select when faced with these choices we would be like demented dogs chasing every attractive smell in complete confusion of purpose. Our ability to make choices depends largely on the quality and range of our imaginal power.* In other words, to make sense of life-situations and to make intelligent decisions when we meet them we need to have pondered the various possibilities either before the situations arise or with speed and sureness when they do arise. For this very reason we are constantly setting up imagined situations in our interior dialogue, our dreams, our talk, so that we can explore various modes of behaviour and the consequences within these prototype circumstances. These explorations may be based on the typical, on the specific (things we have witnessed, re-run and edited in our imaginations like old films), and on actual, known situations we are about to encounter. Children's play is organized thus. Primitive war dances, fertility rites, hunting games and the like are corporate, social enactments. Conversations powered by phrases such as 'Supposing it's this way . . . then . . .' are doing exactly the same job for us. And so does literature. It engages us in imaginal re-enactments; the situations are invented (or described from observation but with editorial refinements for dramatic elegance) by the author and we the readers both observe and get involved in the playing out of the story.

Literature is therefore strongly influential in organizing and sifting the attitudes which inform and guide choice of overt action. I do not mean to say that having read about a character we then go out and behave in a precisely similar fashion. Literature does not programme us to act like robots. Rather it helps clarify, helps bring us to awareness. And whenever we are becoming aware we are, *ipso facto*, in action.

But this is to discuss imaginal action only in relation to circumstances in which we must, or wish to, get involved. There are many we deliberately avoid; and yet they interest us because they are part of human experience. Look, for example, at the fascination murder holds for many people. Few, if any, want to be involved in murder; but that brutal act of one man killing another, his motives for doing so, the personal and social causes and consequences, all hold the attention – as newspaper editors well know. Literature provides a way of participating. We are Raskolnikov in *Crime and Punishment*, and his hunter too. Simenon may be read for amusement only, but if we'll let him he can show a variety of insights into the kind of crises that push people into criminal acts. We may have no belief in God, but through the poetry of Gerard Manley Hopkins

---

* Here and elsewhere in the book I take the term 'imaginal' from I. A. Richards. The reader is referred to his *Practical Criticism*, *Principles of Literary Criticism*, *Coleridge on Imagination*, etc., published by Routledge.

we get into the skin of a man who has, and see with his eyes, think his thoughts, know his belief in both its certainty and its doubt.

Nor is it only great literature that does this for us. Even writing that we reject for its shallowness, its lack of penetration, demands in the very act of rejecting it that we match what we know of life and people against what the writer offers.

All these different ways in which literature functions have enormous value for children. Children are emergent; they are forming attitudes, finding points of reference, building concepts, patterns, images, all of which interact to form a basis for decision-making judgement, for understanding, for sympathy with the human condition. Literary experience feeds the imagination, helping it to come to grips with the astonishing amount of data and experiences which assail children in their daily lives.

'Don't confuse motion with action', Hemingway is said to have advised Miss Dietrich; and he was right. There has been little obvious motion but plenty of action when a child finds through reading a book that a dull day is transformed because he has met a talking water-rat (whom everyone knows is a fiction) telling a talking mole (in whom no one really believes) what a joy it gets from the ordinary river that flows by its quaint but nonexistent front door. And there is more to be gained from an imaginary nineteenth-century American boy floating down the Mississippi on a raft with a fleeing black slave than a good deal of everyday 'direct' experience can give, no matter how much of it is packed into the same time-span as it takes to read *Huckleberry Finn*.

No one but an obsessed fanatic would suggest that reading is all, or enough; but a reader who gets this far doesn't question the value of literature; he knows it. And getting children this far is the first aim of all the work we do with children and books. They won't, many of them, get there on their own: they need help and encouragement, opportunity and guidance; they need to be led to books which will expand their sense of what it means to read fully by methods which do not suffocate the desire to read; and they need to discover that what may be a difficult task is both worth their effort and enjoyable – enjoyable now while they are developing their skills as well as later. After parents, who all too often have not got as far themselves, teachers and librarians more than any other group of people in society carry the responsibility for bringing children and books together. And though they cannot succeed on their own, they are the ones who need to be most aware of what they are doing and how they are doing it when they try and help children grow into literate readers.

References and further reading

1. Richard Hoggart, 'Why I Value Literature' in *Speaking to Each Other*, Volume Two: *About Literature*, Chatto and Windus, 1970, pp. 11ff. Reprinted as Appendix One. My own first chapter is set against the background of this neatly argued general statement, and the two should be read together, though, obviously, Professor Hoggart is not responsible for my inadequacies or conclusions.
2. James Britton, *Language and Learning*, Allen Lane The Penguin Press, 1970. The linguistic development of children examined in carefully organized detail. A brilliant book, the first chapter bears directly on my arguments above, expanding and clarifying points which I have been able to make only in unsubstantiated generalities.
3. C. S. Lewis, *An Experiment in Criticism*, Cambridge University Press, 1961. An attempt to consider literature from the way people read, Lewis's theme throws up important implications about children and their reading as well as being a helpful exploration of the value of literature.
4. Lord David Cecil, 'The Appreciation of Literature' in *The Listener*, 9 December 1971, pp. 797–8. Reprinted as Appendix Two. A mature, wholesome and urbanely worded explication of the literary way of reading, and the way to approach criticism.
5. Kornei Chukovsky, *From Two to Five*, rev. ed., trans. and ed. Miriam Morton, Berkeley, The University of California Press, 1968, distributed in the UK by Cambridge University Press. Pinnacle figure in Russian children's literature, Chukovsky first published his investigation into the language, thought processes and imagination of children in 1925, since when it has become a classic, and, being the work of a poet as well as a scholar, it beguiles as well as instructs. The translation does not do the book credit, but it is still essential reading for anyone who wishes to understand the early linguistic and imaginative needs of children and the value of literature for them.
6. Paul Hazard, *Books, Children and Men*, trans. Marguerite Mitchell, The Horn Book Inc., Boston USA, 1944, distributed in UK by B. F. Stevens and Brown. Hazard, a French Academican, has a lot to say about value of literature, and children's approach to it. An unusual book that strikes a rare balance between wit and high seriousness.
7. Pat D'Arcy, *Reading for Meaning*, two vols., Hutchinson Educational, 1973. Useful survey of recent research and experiments in teaching of reading and the reading responses of children.

TWO

The making of a literary reader

Readers are made, not born. No one comes into the world already disposed for or against words in print. It is not easy, however, to separate out all the complicated circumstances, stages of psychological development, individual idiosyncrasies, and adult and peer influences that interweave and form a child's literary development. But I want in this chapter to try and unravel some of the dominant and generally applicable ramifications which have relevance to the main theme. For clarity's sake I have grouped them under headings; but I cannot stress enough how artificial these categories are. The influences described never work in splendid isolation but interact in varying combinations and strengths depending on an individual's personal history. People are not machines and are never completely alike; discussions of the kind that follow are only useful when we remember this.

Socialization

One of those jargon words invented and enjoyed by sociologists and educational theorists, 'socialization', happens to be more convenient than most and a little less objectionable. The Penguin *Dictionary of Psychology* defines it as 'the process by which the individual is adapted to his social environment, and becomes a recognized, co-operating, and efficient member of it.' That is to say, socialization is the name we give to the way children learn to behave like the people around them, taking for their own the attitudes, values, customs, mores of the social group to which they belong.

What we know about this process has stark implications for our theme. Quite obviously, as most children spend their infant years, which is the important period in socialization, aware of very few people, usually members of their family, it is from them, parents, brothers and sisters, attendant relatives and friends, that they learn the primary adaptive lessons. Naturally, how these people regard books, how much they read and talk about what they read, how many books they buy and borrow, keep about them and value, will be part of the way of life absorbed by their children almost as if by osmosis.

But this is by no means all there is to it. The principal instrument of socialization is speech. The quality of the talk that goes on in a family, especially perhaps at relaxed times during meals, in leisure activities, and before bed, strikes deep, to the roots of a child's proper growth. When the talk is rich in content, topics, anecdotes, sharing of opinions and experiences, when it is spoken in a variety of tones and is verbally colourful and inventive, a child is being prepared for the possibilities of language. Whereas when the talk is limited, anaemic, verbally and tonally narrow, just the opposite is true; a deprivation occurs that will later show itself in difficulties in learning to read, in writing, in coping with social situations where speech is cardinal.

Within this oral tradition the socializing part played by storytelling and reading aloud is central to the encouragement of literacy. Listening to stories, poems, nursery rhymes, nonsense, acclimatizes the infant imagination, while occupied in a comforting activity, to the idea of character, the structuring of events in story, the shape and rhythms of prose and poetry; by it too is nurtured stamina, the focus of attention and concentration which reading calls for. There is no surprise in the increasingly weighty evidence presented in ever more numerous research reports which confirms that children from homes in which books are plentiful, speech rich and reading aloud a commonplace experience tend to look forward to learning to read and indeed frequently arrive at school already able to do so, while children from homes where speech has a narrow range and books are absent tend to be the ones who have difficulty. It is interesting, to take just one such report, that after investigating again four years later the two thousand children originally used in the Plowden Report to see how the intervening period had affected their attainment, the investigators could record that 'The early years tend to set the pattern of all that follows'.* If this seems a somewhat gloomy conclusion, it is cheering to discover that the same report offers 'two pieces of proverbial wisdom – that the child is father to the man and that it is never too late to mend'.

A book-conscious home lays a solid foundation but there are socializing factors which may undermine it and which, of course, further disable those children who lack that basic support. These have been frequently noted and I need only mention them briefly here.

1. Children born into large families or brought up in institutions are at a disadvantage; they have less opportunity than children in small families for sustained conversations *with adults*, and it is speech exchange with mature people that matters in infant years rather than exchanges with other children. Similarly, they have less opportunity to be read to on their own, which has a different

* G. F. Peaker, *The Plowden Children Four Years Later*, National Foundation for Educational Research, 1971.

quality from being read to as one of a group. Thus we can find that seven-year-old children from large families may be on average as much as one year behind those from small families in reading attainment.*

2. Living in overcrowded conditions adversely affects reading progress: there is a lack of quiet, and of private places where children can escape from noise, movement, visitors, TV, to find an atmosphere conducive to reading. Overcrowded houses are frequently a correlate of large families thus exacerbating the problems described above, which are again further compounded if the family is financially poor and linguistically limited. Some 37 per cent of the children of unskilled workers live in cramped homes, a statistic chilling in its educational implications.*

3. No family lives in isolation unless it is remarkably cut off geographically. Spreading out from the doorstep is a wider social group which is brought to bear on the child particularly after he is old enough to wander at large on his own. In *The Uses of Literacy*(1) Richard Hoggart has vividly described the culturally formative power of tightly-knit neighbourhood communities.

All these socializing influences are at work before a child goes to school; yet until quite recently we have behaved as though good teaching in good schools (whatever we conceived that 'good' to consist in) was, if not enough, then the best that could be done to cure the disabilities of verbally impoverished children. Now we have begun to admit, though we have on the whole done little about it, that the early years before a child goes to school may have a permanent, life-long effect, and that if we want to improve 'educational standards' (certainly if we want to make literary readers) with more than minimal speed we must get at the social roots that cause deprivation. In short, education must go home, must involve parents and the conditions in which families live far more intimately than has been achieved ever before except by the wealthy, already articulate and literate few.

There is, however, no reason to despair of schools having an influence on children from illiterate homes even as things still are, otherwise the short history of universal education would be much sorrier than it is. Schools themselves are a socializing agent, and though the children will have already formed before they arrive the basic attitudes which will be important to literacy they are, except in extreme and rather rare cases, far from carapaced beyond penetration. 'It is never too late to mend' says the post-Plowden report, and that is true, provided we keep in mind that whatever goes on in school is set by children against what goes on in their

* Reported in *From Birth to Seven*, A National Child Development Study, 1972.

homes, and that when those two socializing incubators breed in anything but harmony, even by default rather than design, the children in between are disturbed by the discord.

A child's life cannot without impairing consequences be separated into two unconnected compartments in which, on the one side, teachers take no account of home and neighbourhood, and parents, on the other side, know little and understand less about the institution where their child spends a considerable part of his days. Taking as the classic model of this dilemma the 'uprooted and anxious' grammar-school boy from a working-class home, Richard Hoggart has described the far-reaching tensions of such dual existence and includes this passage on the literary side-effects:

> Such a boy is between two worlds of school and home; and they meet at few points. Once at the grammar-school, he quickly learns to make use of a pair of different accents, perhaps even two different apparent characters and differing standards of value. Think of his reading-material, for example: at home he sees strewn around, and reads regularly himself, magazines which are never mentioned at school, which seem not to belong to the world to which school introduces him; at school he hears about and reads books never mentioned at home. When he brings those books into the house they do not take their place with other books which the family are reading, for often there are none or almost none; his books look, rather, like strange tools.
> (1. p. 296)

But this is not a simple equation formulating a relationship between only one specific social class and one specific kind of education; as I pointed out earlier the same double standards are to be found throughout society and all kinds of schools. Children caught between suffer educational schizophrenia. They are moved by natural pressures to dissociate from one or other socializing sphere, or indeed, in the modern adolescent manner, from both, rejecting school and home as equally inadequate. For many children home standards, familiar from infancy, claim if not loyalty then certainly, through deep-seated and compelling emotional ties, unquestioning acquiescence. Other children strike an uneasy balance; and still others struggle to slough off the cultural clothing provided by their upbringing in favour of a different wardrobe taken from school or from peers met in the wider world outside home and neighbourhood.

The implications of this analysis are burdensome, calling out questions which 'have to do with the importance of roots, of unconscious roots, to all of us as individuals; they have to do with those major social developments of our times towards centralization and a kind of classlessness; and they have to do with the relationship between cultural and intellectual matters and the beliefs by which men try to shape their lives.' (1) They are questions which reach beyond the confines of this present book, but they do point to some conclusions we need to take into account.

Firstly, teachers cannot afford to turn a blind eye to the literature a child is brought up with at home no matter how anaemic it may seem to be. It is what the child knows, and 'work from the known to the unknown' is an old pedagogic saw as potent today as ever. When children come from book-conscious homes, this presents no difficulty; school is then hardly more than an extension and intensification of home reading activities. For children from 'nonbook' homes the transition is not so smooth. By discovering what they read – probably comics, cheap pulp books, Christmas annuals, newspapers, and special interest magazines – and by talking about it *from knowledge* (which means we must pay the child the same compliment we expect him to pay us, and read what he tells us about) teacher and pupil find common ground, a point of departure into, for the child, the unfamiliar. So a relationship of trust is forged out of mutual interest and respect which makes a child far more willing to be led where the teacher would take him; and, just as important, the sharp division between home and school is blurred a little and the tensions eased.

Secondly, schools need to make deliberate, carefully planned efforts to awaken parents to the part they play in the literary education of their children by drawing them whenever possible into the work done in school. In areas of chronic illiteracy this may need to be conducted with as much energy as is given to classroom work. We have hardly begun to touch this aspect of educational strategy; and indeed it is a daunting prospect for those teachers who face all the problems endemic in the places where literary impoverishment is most acute, the heavily populated, least prosperous city areas. Nevertheless, through parent–teacher associations, by encouraging parents to come into infant and primary school classrooms to read with their children, by using school bookshops, book fairs, and libraries as centres where teachers, parents and children can meet informally and buy, borrow, and discuss books, by teachers' visits to homes, and by bringing parents into school at regular intervals to discuss their children's reading progress, in fact by any device that can be thought of, a network of opportunities for the kind of exchange that educates the parents as well as their children can be woven into the fabric of the school's daily life, further breaking down the compartmented separation that wreaks so much damage. It would be starry-eyed idealism to believe that we will ever reach into every home in this way; there will always be a depressingly high percentage of intransigent parents, and those perhaps the ones most in need of help, who resist all such overtures. But it is worth remembering that most parents care deeply about their children's education, and will go to

considerable lengths to promote it if they are shown, without con-
descension or imperiousness (both occupational diseases of school-
teachers), what to do and how to do it, *and why*.

Thirdly, because it is the socializing that goes on in pre-school
infancy that matters above all we must, as a society and as teachers
with special responsibilities within that society, do more to put
matters right at this stage instead of waiting until the damage is
done and then trying to rehabilitate those who have suffered, knowing all the while that the evidence we have suggests that we are
fighting against the odds. Prevention is better than cure. We did
not get rid of the plague by treating the illness but by cleaning up
the conditions which bred it. The same will be true of illiteracy and
of literary impoverishment. As a society we are strong on physical
health, providing all kinds of welfare services to help pre- and post-
natally; young mothers and fathers can get advice on everything
from baby food to inoculations, from talcum powders to family
planning. But we are pretty weak on mental and imaginal health;
local child-care clinics and the like are on the whole about as
ignorant in that field as the young mothers and fathers they are
there to help. The authorities have, it seems, assumed that the
provision of free public libraries ought to satisfy the literary needs
of the nation, but the kind of parents we have in mind never pass
through a library's doors. Unless the libraries are as enlightened
and outgoing as, for instance, those in the London Borough of
Lambeth (which is the exception, not the rule), then this 'free'
provision does very little about meeting young parents on their
own ground, in the places where they gather: clinics, play groups,
young wives' associations, welfare offices, not to mention shopping
centres, recreation clubs and the public service departments of
town and city government offices.

Secondary-school teachers can, and some do, play a role in preparing future parents for their responsibilities. It is now commonplace for school leavers to be given courses that touch on topics
bearing on the making and raising of a family. Far from commonplace within those courses, when in fact it ought to be of central
importance, is a study of the linguistic and literary development of
infants. Girls particularly are receptive to such teaching; the subject fascinates them and the content is no less intriguing. Nor
should it be, nor need it be only theoretical; there is plenty of room
for work of a practical and even an experimental nature. And when
the point is reached of discussing (as well as actually doing) story-
telling and reading aloud, of comparing books for very young
children, and thinking about the place in a baby's life of nursery
rhyme and nonsense verse, of pictures and words, of fairy and folk
tales, and when arguing the merits and demerits of comics and toy
books, adolescents can become passionately involved. A nerve has

been touched at a time when young people are prepared to listen, and, hopefully, remember. So it is at this stage that most can be done to make prospective parents understand and prepare for the linguistic needs of the children they will beget.

Quite obviously, however, everything rests in the end on the extent to which people grow up to be avid readers; which brings us back to the role teachers and schools play in that process. And once again fundamental features mark the landscape.

1. Just as non-reading children are made by non-reading parents, so the issue is compounded by non-reading teachers. Unless a school is staffed by people who enjoy books and enjoy talking to children about what they read then it is hardly likely that they will be very successful in helping children to become readers. Lip service (and reading gets plenty of that in educational circles) is not enough. 'Do as I say, not as I do' is an unconvincing dogma.

2. Surroundings matter. Whether or not reading is an activity given space and the kind of physical conditions it requires, how books are presented and displayed as objects, how easily accessible they are: considerations like these, dealt with in detail in later chapters, affect the disposition of children towards books.

3. Furthermore, in the nature of school life there are biases which, if not guarded against or properly handled, turn children away from the goal we seek.

Ironically the most dangerous bias exists because of the usefulness and convenience of books themselves. The printed word in book form even now has no rival as the most efficient, effective, and indeed attractive vehicle by which we teach and learn. Consider the result. Almost every lesson, every school activity relies on the use of books: textbooks – which are no more than teaching machines with at least one for any subject a child is likely to find taught in school – supplementary 'readers', instruction manuals, reference works, tomes teeming with 'problems' to be solved – all these besides a plethora of non-fiction on any and every topic imaginable. If in teaching session after teaching session, day after day, school tasks are administered primarily through books we ought not to be surprised by two logical consequences. First, all but the most avid child readers will want to escape from books and reading in their leisure time. Secondly, because books are so weightily presented as a means of instruction, of fact-finding and didacticism, children too often come to suppose that this is the nature and purpose of all books, that this is how all books must be read, except, of course, for those frothy and outlaw delights like comics and the pulp pleasures which you can tell very easily by the fact that no one ever mentions them, and certainly not approvingly, in school. In short, we can fall into the trap of teaching children only one way of reading: that which seeks the acquisition of information.

4. Out of this fact-grubbing, didactic bias grows another: abuse and misuse of literature. Some examples will best indicate my meaning. I once worked with an English teacher who taught first-year secondary children to parse by setting for sample text the opening paragraph of *Moonfleet*. This extraordinary assault on a fine children's book, popular with many young readers though it never was among those who were ordered to take part in this eccentric act of grammatical rape, epitomizes for me the scholastic abuse of literature. But it is no less misguided, only more crude, than the common malpractice of setting passages thieved from similar sources for comprehension exercises. (What colour was the pirate's coat? How do you know? How many men did the officer have with him? What time of day was it? Why does Joe tell Susan to 'Belt up!'? etc.) Every major English textbook I can think of abuses literature in this treacherous fashion. But this is only the beginning. Close on such parade-ground drills comes the popular sport of plundering for projects. The children are 'doing', let's say, a group project about dogs. They are encouraged to hunt out any-thing and everything that so much as mentions the animals; and the bits thus mined are assiduously transcribed into project folders. We'll be sure not to miss *A Dog So Small*: there are a few sentences about borzois on page 13 and there are all those bits about puppies in Chapter 14. They'll go well with some extracts from the *Observer Book of Dogs*. Naturally, we shall want the fight scene from *White Fang*, and just for fun (and to show how Sir's liberal eye shines on everyone) we'll suggest a squib about William Brown's cur, Jumbles, to put alongside a passage about mongrels from the *World Book Encyclopaedia*. All is raked together into a kind of anthological rag-bag which passes for 'research', for a 'child-centred learning situation'. And it has all been set down without reference to context or author's intention or the difference between one kind of writing (and reading) and another – between the naked facts and figures of the *Observer Book* and Philippa Pearce's re-creation of a flesh-and-blood boy. My picture may seem a parody, may even seem a slur on those teachers who make careful and intelligent use of the project method, and I urgently apologize if it is; but I fear it is not uncommon for children to be encouraged to gather in this undis-criminating manner bits and pieces from every kind of book. What betrays this approach is that children are thus misled as to the true nature and value of literature, treating it as a resource, in the educa-tionally technical sense of that trendy word, rather than as an experience to be entered into, shared and contemplated. It is the difference between 'using' and 'receiving' literature.*

* The distinction is C. S. Lewis's, made in *An Experiment in Criticism*:

5. In parallel with these two biases a third must be weighed, though it shows signs of being counteracted by many teachers: the puritanical narrowness of the 'official literature' presented to children for approved reading and study. In a quite understandable anxiety to give only the best to children, we have too often undermined the very thing we were trying to achieve by interpreting 'the best' as meaning but one kind of writing rather than the best of all kinds. This thought returns us to Hoggart's description of the two standards that confront his working-class grammar-school boy. In the last twenty years a growing number of teachers have challenged this situation. They have examined their own reading habits honestly and drawn unsettling conclusions about what should be expected of children as readers. They have thought through their own development from childhood and acted on the implications this revealed for their work as teachers. They have understood, to begin with, that the traditional 'classics' are not the only texts worth close reading, but that there is a rich body of 'children's books' which merits just as much consideration by adults as by children. They have noted the separation between what they as teachers tend to bring into the classroom and the popular reading done outside school, and have looked for ways of interleaving the two so that the one illuminates the other. Thus it is not difficult these days to find teachers whose lessons draw their pupils into a discussion of *Beano*, *Victor*, Tin-Tin and Asterix, or a Billy Bunter story and William Mayne's *Cathedral Wednesday*, or a 'love' story from *Petticoat* along with Beverly Cleary's *Fifteen* and Paul Zindel's *I Never Loved Your Mind*. They have realized, these teachers, that what matters is not that children should read only those books adults have decided will be 'good for them', but that adults and children together should share all that children can read, do read and should read, looking for the 'good' in it – not only the moral 'good' or the didactic 'good' but the 'good' that is entertaining and revealing, re-creative, re-enactive, and engaging.

Before we leave the socializing process we must note one more factor that will be further considered in a later chapter. From the time children go to school they mix with large numbers of their contemporaries and peers who exert an ever-increasing influence as the school years pass. Some children are swayed more than others by the attitudes, opinions, behaviour of friends and fellows, but none escapes untouched, not even the outsider, the natural loner. And this is something teachers cannot neglect, for it plays an

'A work of (whatever) art can be either "received" or "used". When we "receive" it we exert our senses and imagination and various other powers according to a pattern invented by the artist. When we "use" it we treat it as assistance for our own activities.' (p. 88)

inevitable part in children's corporate and individual responses to them and what they are trying to achieve.

Thus teachers find themselves along with parents and peers one of a triumvirate of main socializing agents in a child's life. Though not necessarily the most important and powerful, they are so placed that they are able to influence the other two, while the responsibility society has put upon them provides opportunities as well as resources which give them advantages over both parents and peers.

Stages of growth

So far I have outlined some of the social conditions which affect a child's reading development; I want now to turn to another aspect: that which has to do with psychological growth. Just as we can recognize stages of physical growth so I believe we can isolate stages of psychological growth that have relevance to our theme. These are at work at the same time as the social influences; they may harmonize or they may clash, but they do not operate separately. A shift in the one will cause a modification in the other; hence we see the infinite number of variations between children of the same age.

What are these stages? What should we expect of children as they pass through them? What do we learn from them about the development of literary taste? As a starting point in answering these questions two authoritative voices can be brought to our aid. The first, Dr Levin Schücking, suggests stages of growth as he has observed them.

> The child's intelligence as it first begins to develop is most easily attracted by the description of familiar day-to-day incidents, usually regarding its own life; when its imagination awakes, without corresponding development of the critical faculty, it gets a taste for fairy stories; with the awakening of youthful urge to activity it finds fascination in tales of adventure; puberty brings interest in the dreamy and sentimental; maturity brings a more realistic make-up; greater experience of life and the growing sense of reality bring a dislike of highly coloured representation of things and a preference for keen and satirical observation over the merely fanciful. Most adults feel the awakening of interest in biography and a diminution at the same time of the fondness for fiction. (2. p. 78)

This brief sketch is enlarged by Jacqueline Burgoyne, who adds details noted by other students of reading growth and confirmed by her own investigations.

> Schücking suggests stages in reading development to which we have added another intermediate stage because Schucking was concerned only with literary development. He suggests that a young child is first attracted to reading by finding that the real world which he has so far

perceived and experienced can also be found in stories and books. At this stage children like stories to be about themselves and the things which they have experienced, and a child's very first books may consist only of illustrations and text describing familiar incidents, as the first 'Ladybird' books do. At this stage pictures are important; they link visual and verbal symbols and their importance declines as the child grasps more of the symbolic significance of words and is able to build up his own imaginative pictures from verbal stimulus. Words describe more explicitly yet leave the imagination free to work and in adult books illustrations, unless they have an aesthetic appeal, are included only where a diagram would be shorthand for a longer verbal explanation.

A second stage, Shücking suggests, is reached at the time at which the young child's powers of imagination are very active. He has begun to perceive experience beyond the home and local environment and to conceive of processes and emotions more exciting than everyday life; this is the world of fancies, Santa Claus, 'human' animals like Winnie the Pooh and Peter Rabbit, and Daleks and is often shown by the way in which a young child is able to carry on a sustained relationship with an imaginary friend or animal. At this stage schools recognize that much is learned through play; new roles are tried out and a child begins to enter imaginatively into other worlds. Stories and books are an important part of this process.

The development of imaginative powers and perception is not uniform; we all know adults whom we consider unimaginative or perhaps over-imaginative and little is known about the way in which these differences occur. Studies of deprived children suggest that those who do not receive the necessary stimulus in early childhood may never be able to compensate. In one sense learning is a chain process; we hang a new piece of knowledge, technique of doing or thinking on something learned previously. If the first links are missing it is difficult for schools to make good the deficiencies.

Schücking stresses that at this stage 'imagination flows without critical faculty'. This is when children are not really concerned with scientific truth; they believe in Father Christmas anyway, even if there lurks the suspicion that there is something rather fishy about it all. Perhaps an openly expressed disbelief in his activities is one of the marks of the passing of this stage.

At the next step facts become increasingly important. Teaching methods which stress 'finding out' and personal discovery are based upon a thesis of Piaget's, a Swiss psychologist, that at this stage of 'concrete operations' children think in factual terms which are an essential preliminary to abstract and deductive thought. Although some children will have already become inveterate readers, in their spare time up until puberty activity is generally more important than reflective thinking. It is possible that this is why historical writers such as Rosemary Sutcliff and Alfred Duggan are so popular at this stage; fantasy is linked with factual material and much modern fiction for this age is increasingly realistic, for example, the writing of J. Rowe Townsend and William Mayne. This period of latency, where, if Freud's framework is valid, emotion plays a relatively small part, is disregarded by Shücking because this may be the time when children are least interested in works of a literary nature.

Puberty, he describes as 'dreamy and sentimental' and though this may seem a far cry from the teenagers of the 1960's, we would recognize that adolescence brings an awakening of emotions, idealism and commitment to a romantic ideal. For those who are active readers there is plenty to read and teachers have commented to us upon the amount and diversity of reading done by 'readers', more often girls than boys. In one term this may vary from Jane Austen to Alan Sillitoe, Hardy and Scott to Margaret Drabble, with a regular dose of *Valentine* thrown in.

By adolescence the die is usually cast and those who never read rarely come to find pleasure in reading in itself, although they may be helped toward a more mature use of books for the extension of other activities. . . .

Perhaps we should make a distinction at this stage between fiction which comforts, reinforcing the reader's ideas and values, or provides him with an escape from the dull real world where people rarely 'live happily ever after' and fiction which challenges readers to think and to face reality. Teenage escape reading is often found through magazines.

Transition to maturity is characterized by Shücking as a 'dislike for highly coloured representations' as a result of greater experience of life and a growing sense of reality. This results, he says, 'in an awakening of interest in biography and a diminution at the same time of fondness for fiction'. This is certainly true of a large number of readers, although the transition is rarely absolute. We continue to enjoy a certain number of books whose only purpose is distraction, but they are not our complete diet. (3. pp. 43–47)

These two synoptic passages serve as introduction; but there are modifiers to be added at a number of points.

1. It would be a mistake to suppose that these broad stages of development precisely correspond to clear-cut chronological or 'reading' ages. That they do not raises difficulties for teachers faced with large groups of children who, though they may be the same age within a year, will certainly differ greatly in their stages of reading development. The principle we can adopt to ease the problem is that we should provide in school at least as much opportunity, if not more, for individual reading and individual response between teacher and child as for corporate. And these opportunities must be offered against a background of book-stocks that are themselves catholic in range and appeal, both in kind so that they satisfy different stages of development and in 'reading age' so that they span the spectrum of attainment.

2. The stages are not cut off from one another but rather they overlap, and sometimes even rub along together. A child may enjoy *Winnie-the-Pooh* and Peter Rabbit and at the same time show a strong interest in factual information which, according to Schücking's model, would predominate at a later stage of

development. Equally, children may 'relapse' for a while, returning to a stage they appeared to have left behind. And in pubescence especially they frequently oscillate, reaching at one moment way ahead of themselves towards mature adult books and diving back at another moment into favourite books that belong to an earlier stage of their growth. These shifts of emphasis have various causes: a change of friends, for instance, may realign a child's reading interests so that they suit the new relationship; an emotional crisis at home may send him burrowing back into the security of well-loved books remembered from happier days; a new and attractive teacher may accelerate progress from one stage to another. Clearly, the more teachers know about the children in their charge the better equipped they are to judge not only the reasons for such fluctuations but how to respond helpfully.

3. Far more concerning than fluctuations about the main thrust of growth is arrested development when a person gets 'stuck' at one stage. Many women, for example, never grow as readers beyond the pubescent proclivity for 'dreamy and sentimental' narrative, as the popularity of women's magazines, 'true romance' stories and Mills and Boon novels demonstrate. Men, for their part, will often ossify at the adventure stage when Biggles holds imagination in check. James Bond, dashing thrillers and war stories belong to this family tree. 'Such people,' Schücking says 'are in certain respects incapable of progressing beyond the impressions belonging to a period in their lives when their minds were open and receptive to things of this kind. In later years, however, their enjoyment of art is all too often nothing but their own youth which their memory enables them to enjoy all over again.'* There is of course plenty of evidence to suggest that the period when factual information makes its strongest appeal and when literary reading is at its lowest ebb is the stage at which most people are arrested. I wonder if this is not altogether unrelated to the fact that this stage immediately precedes puberty, during the last flush of childhood, after which, as secondary school teachers know too well, children commonly experience a conscious disenchantment with adults and institutions that for want of a better target they direct at teachers and schools. Children cannot then be led so easily, so unselfconsciously as before the onset of adolescence, and disenchantment can be a door that closes tight against attempts to refurbish dulled literary receptivity.

4. Miss Burgoyne distinguishes between books which comfort and confirm and those which challenge and subvert. But to make the distinction in this simplistic equation is misleading because it suggests that books are willy-nilly of two kinds only, each possessing intrinsic, absolute qualities which inevitably affect readers in one way or the other. And this is not the case. I touched upon this

* (2. p. 79)

aspect of literature in the previous chapter and quoted Lionel Trilling's remarks about *Huckleberry Finn*. If we look again at this passage (p. 11) we will see that Trilling claims this novel 'is indeed a subversive book', but he adds an essential qualifying clause: 'no one who reads thoughtfully the dialectic of Huck's great moral crisis. . . .' In other words, the subversive effect of the book depends entirely on how the reader reads. Fully received by a person open to its irony, aware of its devastating incisiveness and willing to set its moral dialectic against himself, the book is challenging, as Trilling says it is and Twain intended. But it is quite possible for someone to read the story as a vastly entertaining collection of picaresque adventures written with consummate stylistic skill and full of 'colourful' characters, yet for his own prejudices, beliefs and customary morality to remain untouched by Huck's crisis and Twain's intention in exploring it. Both readers would agree on the literary quality of the work, but its effects on them would be quite different.

Similarly, as I hinted in the previous chapter, the most mediocre of books, the ones which will not bear close attention because they are conventional, clichéd, expressive of tired prejudices, and good for nothing but a cheap thrill or a rosy-tinted day-dream, can still challenge a 'thoughtful' reader. Not, it is true, by intention, but because he who knows how to read with a fully receptive response will recognize the deficiencies of shallow mediocrity and reject the sham; but in so doing he must exercise judgements which call in question his attitudes, beliefs, knowledge and prejudices. This is not to say such a reader always scorns inadequate literature with judicial solemnity; on the contrary, he may enjoy it heartily, as one can enjoy hammy acting or candy-floss or inconsequential banter. But he knows it for what it is.

The knowing is what matters. A reader who is never challenged, unsettled or moved, who has never realized how books can be – intentionally or otherwise – subversive, is a reader who does not know. He does not know how to receive literature, does not know how to discover his responses or how to express them to himself and others.

So we reach the final stage in the making of a literary reader. Schücking noted that early step when a child's 'imagination awakes, without corresponding development of the critical faculty', a step most children make before they reach school age (and which, to be pessimistic, most people seem never to get beyond). Awakening the critical faculty is therefore part of what the 'direct' teaching of literature is all about. It is pointless, as David Holbrook among many others has observed, to 'make bookworms who will later bore only through pulp.' It is not enough to get children reading regularly and often, though this is where literary reading begins; not enough, either, to get them reading books of great quality, though this must itself be a goal. What ultimately matters is that children be brought to a valued appreciation that reading is more than a passive pursuit – 'Here I am: amuse me!' – but is a creative activity, an end in itself, yielding many pleasures simultaneously.

Much has been written about teaching methods directed at making children critically appreciative readers, and as I explained in my Preface the subject lies outside the purview of this book. But one thing I do want to say so as to avoid misunderstanding. By teaching children to be critical I do not mean teaching them to pull books apart in an act of cold-blooded and mechanically formulated analysis, as though they were dismantling a piece of machinery, an act that ends with the making of comparative judgements about this book being 'better' than that, or one writer being greater than another. Helen Gardner, no mean teacher and no mean critic herself, has summed up what needs to be said about such misguided practice.

> The attempt to train young people in this kind of discrimination seems to me to be a folly, if not a crime. The young need, on the one hand, to be encouraged to read for themselves, widely, voraciously, and indiscriminately; and, on the other, to be helped to read with more enjoyment and understanding what their teachers have found to be of value. Exuberance and enthusiasm are proper to the young, as Quintillian remarked: 'The young should be daring and inventive and should rejoice in their inventions, even though correctness and severity are still to be acquired.' And he added that to his mind 'the boy who gives least promise is one in whom judgement develops in advance of the imagination'. True personal discrimination or taste develops slowly and probably best unconsciously. It cannot be forced by exercises in selecting the good and rejecting the bad by the application of stock critical formulas: it may indeed be stunted. It comes, if it is to come at all, by growth in understanding and enjoyment of the good. 'Principium veritatis admirari.' Knowledge begins in wonder and wonder will find and develop its own proper discipline. True judgement or wisdom in a critic can only come in the same way as all wisdom does: 'For the very true beginning of her is the desire of discipline and the care of discipline is love.'*

The art of teaching literature so that young people become critically aware, of helping them, as Helen Gardner puts it, 'to read with more enjoyment and understanding what their teachers have found to be of value', is a specialist concern.

> The plain fact is that every teacher cannot deal with literature and we must not expect every teacher to deal with it. Most teachers, with

---

* Helen Gardner, *The Business of Criticism*, Oxford University Press paperbacks, 1963, pp. 13–14; by permission of The Clarendon Press, Oxford.

proper preparation, could give very effective lessons in arithmetic and 'information' subjects; but no quantity of preparation will enable those teachers to make the literature lessons anything but a dismal failure, if they have not a genuine gift of transmissable appreciation. Unfortunately most of our teachers . . . are so extraordinarily efficient that they do not know their limitations . . . and they would resent a suggestion that they should leave literature alone in schools. But a simple test should convince them. Do they themselves habitually turn to the world's best literature for their own daily refreshment, pleasure or consolation? Do they find in great poetry and prose of the past and the adventurous poetry and prose of the present the real challenging call of soul to soul? If so, they will probably be very safe persons to pass on to their pupils the torch still burning. But if for them literature is a 'subject', like geography or history, something that has to be studied or 'got up' from a text book, something to be acquired by means of copious annotation and analysis, and laid aside when examinations are over, then I say such teachers have not the ear for literature and must no more attempt to teach it in school than the tone-deaf teacher must attempt to teach music. There is no crime in not having the ear for literature or music; the crime is lacking the ear and persisting in spoiling the song. (4. pp. 105–106)

But this is only one part, and not the greater part, of making children into literate readers. What is much more essential is that they be 'encouraged to read for themselves, widely, voraciously, and indiscriminately'. Every teacher not only can but ought to be deeply involved in offering encouragement. And this is the fundamental aspect of children and reading that concerns us in this book.

References and further reading

1. Richard Hoggart, *The Uses of Literacy*, Chatto and Windus, 1957, Penguin Books 1958. Seminal study of 'changes in working-class culture during the last thirty or forty years, in particular as they are being encouraged by mass publications', still pertinent and absorbing to read.
2. Levin L. Schücking, *The Sociology of Literary Taste*, Routledge and Kegan Paul, 2nd ed. 1966. First published in Germany in 1923, this is an unusual examination of the formation of taste by focusing on the social influences brought to bear on works of art and people's response to them.
3. Peter H. Mann and Jacqueline L. Burgoyne, *Books and Reading*, André Deutsch, 1969. The first of three reports prepared for the Booksellers Association after research into such questions as: What sort of books do people read? What sort of people read books? And why do they read them? Do they buy them or borrow them? The second report – Peter H. Mann, *Books: Buyers*

and Borrowers, André Deutsch, 1971 – looks into how books are brought to people's notice, how book buyers behave, what the differences are between book borrowers and book buyers, and the like. At the time of writing, the third report is yet to appear. Clearly such studies as these have important things to say to teachers concerned about how children become readers and how to encourage reading of literature.

4. George Sampson, *English for the English*, Cambridge University Press, 'New Edition' 1952. Though first published in 1921 and in some respects now out of date, the broad premises of this book hold good, Sampson's suggestions and comments incisive and accurate. Inspirational, stimulating, balanced: worth far more attention than many of the modern attempts to do the same job. With special regard to this chapter, the section titled 'A Programme' has particular relevance.

5. R. F. Dearden, P. H. Hirst and R. S. Peters (eds.), *Education and the Development of Reason*, Routledge and Kegan Paul, 1972. A collection of unevenly useful essays, but the following are apposite to this chapter: P. A. White, 'Socialization and Education', pp. 113; R. F. Dearden, 'Education as a Process of Growth', pp. 65; R. W. Hepburn, 'The Arts and the Education of Feeling and Emotion', pp. 484.

6. Richard M. Jones, *Fantasy and Feeling in Education*, University of London Press, 1968, Penguin Books, 1972. The stages of child development described with particular emphasis placed on the contribution made by fantasy, dreams and the imagination.

THREE

The set and the setting

One day a middle-aged mother discovered that her teenage daughter sometimes smoked pot with friends after school. Distressed, anxious, a little angry, she at first decided to confront her daughter and put a stop to the clandestine affair at once, brooking no argument. On calmer reflection, however, she thought a more reasonable and reasoning approach would be better. After all, she told herself, what did she know about smoking pot? She had never experienced it, and expert opinion about its dangers and effects were contradictory. Besides, her daughter was sixteen, a child no longer; surely it would be better to talk the matter over and try and reach some kind of understanding?

That evening the girl made no bones about the fact that she had taken the drug, and during the ensuing conversation said again and again that without trying it no one could possibly appreciate the attractions of cannabis. Very well, said the mother at last, in that case she would discover what it was like for herself. And she proposed that after school next day the girls should come to the house and allow her to join them in smoking pot. The daughter agreed, and the meeting took place as planned with predictable results: this superficially admirable attempt at mutual understanding through shared experience was a complete flop. Apart from the fact that cannabis often shows no appreciable effects the first time it is taken, two important factors in the situation made failure likely: the participants were in the wrong frame of mind to enjoy what they were doing; and the surroundings were not conducive to the experience. The girls were wary, nervously self-conscious, quite unable to behave naturally. The mother, a little afraid and expecting the worst, was unsettled, despite all her efforts to be open-minded, by her preconceptions not only about the drug but about the rights and wrongs of the position she found herself in. And, making matters worse, this uncomfortable group sat in a suburban sitting-room flooded with afternoon sunlight like dutifully polite members of a formal tea party. Not surprisingly, the girls went away embarrassed, while the mother, if she was any better informed, was certainly none the wiser.

The two factors which predetermined failure in this unhappy story attend the outcome of every human activity, social and private, from lazy picnics during holidays to major crises at work.

Borrowing terms from the psychologists, I want to call them the 'set' and the 'setting'. By the set I mean that mixture of mental and emotional attitudes people bring to the things they do: their expectations, previous experience and knowledge, present moods, relationships with other participants. The setting is the physical surroundings in which an activity takes place.

Thus, a picnic can be a disaster simply because one dominant member of the group is set against it – is feeling bloody-minded we might say – because he is there out of a sense of duty, rather dislikes the others, and generally cannot abide eating outside anyway. And no matter how set everyone is to have a good time, it is difficult for them to do more than make the cheerful best of things if the picnic is held, for some crazy reason, on a stinking rubbish tip in pouring rain: the setting is not favourable. On the other hand people passionately devoted to a hobby or sport or their work will endure without complaint conditions which less ardent folk think outrageously insupportable. So we see extraordinary hardships cheerfully borne (indeed, apparently enjoyed) by zealous mountaineers, earnest single-handed yachtsmen floating round the world, and three million or so all-weather fishing hobbyists who, weekend after weekend, sit patiently at the side of and sometimes in British rivers, undeterred by the paucity of the catches they land. Which leaves unmentioned the crowds of people who, because they are 'on holiday', placidly accept treatment and conditions they would angrily attack as being barbaric at all other times in their lives. Set, it seems, is a more powerful influence than setting; but both play their part and in fact modify each other in forming behaviour.

Reading is no different in this regard from anything else. Come to it willingly, seeking many kinds of pleasure from books, and you soon find enjoyment; but have it foisted on you as a duty, a task to be put-up-with, from which you expect no delight, and it appears a drab business gladly to be given up. Settle down somewhere pleasant and quiet and you can read for hours; do the same where numerous momentary distractions constantly interrupt your attention and even the most willing reader will feel like giving up after a short time. For me personally, the picture of myself in a dentist's waiting room is a perfect metaphor for a set and setting very much in play against the usually easy pleasure I get from reading.

Obviously then, anything we say about introducing books to children must always be accompanied by an understanding that the set of the teacher and children involved and the setting in which they meet and work will make their own contributions to the success of whatever methods are used. Everything said in the rest of this book must be placed in this context. And in order to explore set and setting further, I shall consider them separately, despite

their symbiotic relationship, beginning with the setting because it is
the condition most easily probed and regulated.

The setting

Two things must be carefully kept apart in our minds: the places
where books can be found if and when children want them, and
the conditions in which teachers introduce books to children.
As to the first, I have no doubts or difficulties. The ideal, which we
are laughably far from attaining, is that books should be spread
with prodigal generosity throughout the community: wherever
people go, there they also should be. This may sound like the
pipe-dream of a dyed-in-the-word fanatic; but surely it is no more
than educational common sense when we are thinking about books
in schools? Certainly the last thing we want is that books be shut up
in tastefully decorated warehouses, watched over by highly trained
storekeepers whose main purpose is to see that everything is kept
tidily in its place and, as far as possible, untouched by human
hands – especially the sticky-fingered hands of marauding children.

But what are the *minimal* provisions in the setting which every
school ought to provide in order to encourage in its children (and its
teachers) a desire to read and facilities that make reading possible?
1. Collections of books should be sited and attractively presented
   in all work and leisure areas, not forgetting the staff-room.
2. Some areas (note the plural), open at all times, should be made
   over and properly furnished specifically for people who want to
   read undisturbed. The habit in infant and primary schools of
   organizing reading corners in classrooms might with benefit be
   imported into secondary schools.
3. Book-promotional displays should occupy key sites in the
   building. Chapter five deals with this in detail.
4. There should be some arrangement for selling books, preferably
   through a school bookshop, no matter how minuscule. See
   chapter eight.
5. It should go without saying these days that a school's own
   library ought to be active, inspirational, and central in the
   formal and informal life of staff and pupils.

These seem to me to be the permanent features which are necessary
in providing a background setting for children. When we come,
however, to the art of introducing particular books to particular
children at times and in places often arbitrarily specified by a time-
table then fresh concerns arise, to which the following catechism
has always been for me a useful guide.

1. What kind of surroundings would best suit the book (or
books) I have in mind and the methods I intend to use in introducing them? Clearly, dramatic improvisation based on a story or

poem needs space, whereas a story-telling session with a group of infant children can happen in a small room full of furniture.

2. Will the session be formal or informal? Will the children be seated as an 'audience' facing a 'performer', or as a group, each member of which is to participate? Will everyone be sufficiently comfortable to avoid 'shuffling and distraction but not so comfortable that sleep overtakes lively attention? The aim is to find a grouping which promotes the plans we have in mind and does not hinder them.

3. What will the children be able to see when seated? What do I want them to see? Where is the main source of light? Windows are a trap for the unwary, not just because whatever can be seen through them is a natural focus of attention, but because anyone who has to be looked at and is in front of them is seen as hardly more than a silhouette and is a strain on the eyes.

4. What is the temperature? Too much heat like too much cold dulls the mind. If possible, regulate the temperature before the session begins. Is the room ventilated? Classrooms soon become very stuffy.

5. How good are the acoustics? How much projection is needed to reach the person who will be farthest away? Are there 'dead' spots? (I once worked in a school hall where, in the very centre, a voice from the front was a gabble no matter how loudly or softly spoken. There was also a spot from which, if you struck the floor with a hard rap, you could count the echoing reverberations as the sound bounced from ceiling to wall to floor and back again. The building was a new one.) Can anything be done easily to correct weaknesses? Is it best to group the children in one part instead of others? Sometimes, in large rooms with poor acoustics, some display stands (which can be further employed, see 9 below) put up round the area used will help deaden echoes and allow people to speak more naturally and quietly.

6. How likely is the session to be interrupted? Can this be prevented, or at least arranged to fit my convenience? School welfare services especially – medical people, careers officers, and the like – now seem in many schools to have *carte blanche* to take children from classes as and when they please. Collusion with a helpful secretary will sometimes ward off such intrusions; a child sacrificed for the good of the whole and placed outside to defend the door is a desperate last resort. There is little more destructive of a well-planned and conducted lesson than interruption at its high points. The effect is the same as it would be on a play performance if a theatre manager came on stage during a play and asked for the owner of car number . . .

7. At what time of day will the session take place? And what is the weather like? Children's responses vary according to both.

Small children settle easily to a story-telling at night before bed but are less well disposed just after getting up in the morning, and the same differences are noticeable in school. Late in the afternoon on Friday needs an approach that might not work early on Monday morning. A chilly, rain-soaked day can make a class unpleasantly irritable by mid-afternoon. We cannot alter such conditions, rather they alter the approaches we make to children and what we expect of them.

8. What is the physical state of the books to be handled by the children? How familiar are they with the books themselves? Bright new copies of an unknown book naturally excite more attention than old 'readers' soiled from over-use.

9. What is the decorative state of the room? Will it help or hinder? What can be done, quickly and temporarily if this is the only way, to improve matters? Echoing classrooms with bare walls and stark rows of desks do little to encourage favourable sets. Fortunately books are themselves decorative; they do, as the man said, furnish a room. And allied material is fairly easy to come by – posters, publishers' promotion displays, child-produced drawings, models, etc. A stock kept ready for immediate use is well worth preparing. And display stands of very light construction that can be prepared beforehand and taken to the site of a lesson at the last minute are fairly easily available these days.

'If you're going to play cricket as badly as you do,' a sports teacher used to tell me, 'at least dress like a cricketer.' He knew what he was talking about. It isn't just a matter of looks, of convention and uniformity and putting on a good show. Dressing up like a cricketer, he knew, made you *feel* like one, and feeling like one gave you more confidence so that you played as best you could, even if that was badly. And if a thing's worth doing, as Chesterton rightly said, it is worth doing badly, should that be the only way you can do it. Actors know the difference costume and setting make to performance, the sense of occasion they help create. And these things hold true for teachers and children. The more care we take to prepare attractive surroundings that help our work, the more effective our work will be.

The set

A child's set about books and reading may be deeply ingrained as a result of his experiences with them, or it may be temporary and changeable. We have already come across some of the factors which help to create ingrained sets but we must note them again.

1. The two previous chapters have emphasized how the early experiences with books and reading help to create attitudes and

expectations. When these are favourable, a teacher can build on them with the child's cooperation; otherwise there are barriers to be broken down before progress is made.

2. Wounding difficulties when learning how to read can build antagonistic sets. These may come from poor teaching, frequent absence from school during this stage, physical disabilities of the eyes which are not diagnosed until too late, or emotional disorders unrelated to reading itself but which cause difficulties.

3. Because, as I noted before, books are so much at the heart not of 'education' but 'the process of education' – one of the essential tools – children quickly learn to regard them as a symbol of everything bound up with school life. And those who are made to think themselves failures because of the hammer-blow terms like dull, backward, retarded, underprivileged, disadvantaged, handicapped, less able, slow, rejected, remedial, reluctant, disturbed (we have an amazing armoury of diminishing terms to apply which fool no one, least of all the children they label) not unnaturally snipe back self-protectively by unloading onto the symbol all the things they do not like, including their sense of inadequacy, and then reject as unnecessary to themselves and their desires everything associated with the symbol. Reading becomes an activity for intellectuals – 'clever people' – only. A sixteen-year-old boy said to me on the day he left school, 'I'd read a lot if I was clever, but I'm not, so it isn't worth the bother, is it?' In that one comment is hidden the tragic result of the induced attitude – the set – I'm trying to describe. The spiral begins its downward swirl very early in life: a child has difficulty learning to read, this puts him back in all his other school work, and because he falls behind he is labelled by a term of educational jargon verging on abuse; and this is dispiriting, makes him feel somehow inadequate, deficient – and all because of words in print, through which his troubles began. Children in this state are in a crisis of confidence from which they must be retrieved before their set about books can be refreshed and enlivened.

4. Children suffering from emotional or mental strains may lack the kind of concentration reading demands. The extreme form is seen in people who need medical aid; but there are milder forms as well: these are the periodic times of strain we regard as healthy and normal, like blue moods and fits of depression. The effects are the same but different in intensity: first the desire to read is sapped, then the will, and finally the stamina to tackle anything but short and immediately useful passages of print. Here again we are directed to the importance of knowing the children we teach. It is frequently lack of knowledge that causes teachers to accuse children of being lazy, uncooperative, insubordinate, rude, or plain daft, when even a slight investigation of their living circumstances would reveal very good reasons for their behaviour. Once we

understand a child's prevailing set we are better equipped to decide on the strategy and tactics needed to improve it. We can judge when to be firm and involved, when to leave alone for a while, when to insist and correct, when to employ this method or that. Without such knowledge we are rather like a doctor who treats only symptoms and acts on guesswork, inquiring neither into the cause of an ailment nor its history.

5. I have already gone into the adverse sets created by misuse of books: the effects of monotony, drilling, meaningless drudgery passed off as 'studying literature'. 'Each new experience,' says the Plowden report, 'reorganizes, however slightly, the structure of the mind and contributes to the child's world picture.' But experience is a two-edged sword – it cuts both ways. Let another voice sum it up for me this time. Edward Blishen, writing in the *Times Educational Supplement* about teaching fiction:

> The rule, I believe, is quite simply: *We must never use fiction formally for exercises and pieces of study of this kind.* [He has mentioned tests of understanding, tests of vocabulary, formal tests of understanding of literary devices, literary forms, characterization.] Oh, how much more liberal, more daring, how much broader we now are in the matter of fiction to be examined in the classroom. So here we are analysing Alan Sillitoe, William Golding, Barry Hines. But these feats of fundamentally anxious analysis, the writing of little essays and answering of little questions, they all, for so many young people, spell ultimately a kind of distaste, a shrinking away, for a lifetime, perhaps. Because in this way a work of fiction becomes an element in that schoolish pattern of always anxious analysis: the anxiety being that you are under test all the time. And the association with fiction of anxiety and of any kind of testing must, for all but the specialists (and sometimes for them, if their specialism is imposed), be destructive of the appetite for fiction.*

Sets which become deep-rooted are not upset in a moment: neither the favourable nor the unfavourable. There is no formula prescription, no simple panacea which will revive damaged sensibilities. This is something quite different, however, from momentary deviations from a consistent set. Children no less than adults are subject to bouts of irritation, to times when they feel glum or restless and everything they usually enjoy lacks any attraction, purpose or pleasure. And transitory circumstances in daily life cause these shifts. The difficulty for teachers, whose work is in part determined by specified times when it must be done, is that they cannot just duck away when children are set against what needs to be done. Indeed, many of the circumstances which create unfavourable sets are inherent in the conditions under which children are

* Edward Blishen, 'Learning to love it', *Times Educational Supplement*, 7 July 1972.

taught. We must therefore take into account this phenomenon and be prepared to tackle it.

We can group the most common unsettling influences under headings.

PHYSICAL SURROUNDINGS
These have been discussed in the first part of this chapter.

CONDITIONS IMMEDIATELY BEFOREHAND
Children come into a lesson from something else. What they have been doing, how they have been doing it, produce psychological states which show themselves in the 'mood' they bring to the new activity. Coming from an exciting game on the sports field, for instance, hardly dry from showers, children often are in an agitated frame of mind. They are chattery, still occupied with the game, perhaps not yet ready to engage at once in something that demands, say, silent and calm concentration. Faced by this situation a teacher who launches into the presentation of a new book without first transposing the children's prevailing set into a key that harmonizes with the tune he wants to play courts disaster and will conduct his lesson in discord. Similarly, a class – or a child – that has been involved in a telling-off for any one of the myriad trivial transgressions their flesh is heir to, from talking too loudly in a corridor to baiting an incompetent member of staff (who probably deserved all he got), can arrive at their next lesson in an aggressively uncooperative disposition or a little giggly. On the other hand, they can come from a well-taught science lesson as devoted to the search for scientific truth as a research professor and thus be so mentally and emotionally set upon that course, that any abrupt, unsympathetic attempt to switch them onto a track taking them in another direction will as surely derail them as would the sudden reversal of an express train. It can be quite as difficult to take over from a brilliant teacher as from an incompetent one, if not worse. Such examples could be enumerated endlessly. The point is that no session with children can be properly planned and begun without some thought being given to the prior events that have shaped the children's momentary set. And this means, of course, that a teacher must have enough skill and confidence to improvise when he discovers an unexpected 'mood' as the children enter his lesson.

FORTHCOMING EVENTS
Just as prior circumstances are dispositional, so are prospective ones. These may be regular and seasonal, like Christmas, and school holidays; occasional and minor, like sports matches. The onset of examinations, particularly important 'public' exams, has a dis-

turbing effect, and so does the approach of school leaving, either for another school stage or for good and all. Children involved in important public occasions (and 'important' must be judged from the child's point of view not the adult's) are often not 'themselves' beforehand – occasions like school play performances, orchestral and choir concerts, etc. The arrival of the school doctor or dentist can act on children like smoke on bees: it excites them so that they give up work and may even think of leaving the hive. Again, the catalogue could be endless, and we must plan as best we can for known events while contriving to improvise when, as often happens, such stirring distractions occur unannounced. Indeed, the ultimate test of the good teacher is the success with which he can re-involve his children in the work-in-hand, not after the termly fire practice which everyone knew about well in advance, but rather after the sudden entry without warning of an irate caretaker hot on the scent of the boy who hid his favourite duster during morning break.

ADULTS' AND PEERS' ATTITUDES AT PARTICULAR TIMES
These may be attitudes about current work – books being read, for example – or attitudes to the school generally. Senior classes who have grown into book-consciousness infect junior classes with some of their enthusiasm, for example. A school in which there is internecine strife, producing cliques among staff and children, finds discord reflected in class work, with children responding to teachers they 'like' and support while they obstruct those they 'dislike' and oppose. Peers who are admired, for whatever reasons, tend to be copied and followed, a phenomenon seen on a larger scale outside school when children idolize hero figures like pop stars and football players.

ANTICIPATION
This is a predisposing influence based upon past and present experience which makes people look forward to doing something, or the contrary. A skilled teacher can create a pleasant sense of anticipation, a desire to go to his lessons, both by the very fact that he is skilled (children tend to admire people who do things well and are usually very astute about the skill of those who teach them), and because part of his skill lies in an ability to prepare for what is to come, leading pupils on all the time. We've all heard children say such things as: 'I like English because Mr Jones makes it interesting.'

BILLY BUNTER, WILLIAM BROWN AND FLASHMAN
The comic butt, the natural-born leader, and the bully: representative, archetypal figures, patterns of which are to be found in most

groups of children. I mention them here to remind us that there are personalities in any collection of people who are at one and the same time barometers indicating the climate within the social group they tend to dominate, and weather-makers determining the climate. On the attitudes and behaviour of key children can depend the sets which rule those they influence. We must discover not only how to monitor these influences but also how to disarm them when they are adverse and encourage them when they are favourable.

I have spoken in general of temporary sets in relation to group responses, but I hope it is obvious that individuals within groups experience sets peculiar to their personal condition at certain times. Thus there is usually at least one child whose current set runs counter to the prevailing group set. A class may be keen, alert, contributive, except for one child who is withdrawn, distracted, unresponsive. He faces a teacher with an eternal problem: how far does one go in turning a blind eye, leaving him alone? Should a teacher *always* attempt to engage such a child's attention and interest? Should he be firm and persistent? It is at this point that many factors come into play: the teacher's experience, judgement, knowledge of the child. There is no suitable generalization to be made, except, perhaps, to say that any attempt to coerce a response without good reason based upon that child's present circumstances is to place in jeopardy not only that one child's willing engagement now and in the future, but the prevailing favourable set and attention of the rest of the group. A lesson all teachers have to learn is that they cannot carry all children with them all the time; one session is not the be-all and end-all of their work. Literary readers are not made in a day, but grow, develop, mature over years. Nor is this growth, as we have said before, steadily progressive, like a car on an assembly line, bit being added after bit with smooth, robot efficiency. Rather, readers grow by fits and starts, now rushing ahead, now lying fallow, and now moving steadily on. In the day-to-day practice of his art it is easy for a teacher to lose sight of that overall truth and think he personally is failing when all that is happening is that a child is following a perfectly natural, if erratic, path.

FOUR

Story-telling and reading aloud

The oral tradition – stories told aloud – goes right back to primitive
man, to the tribe and its communal life. And still today, though
there are many people who say they do not enjoy or have no time
for literary reading, I have yet to meet anyone who does not like
hearing a story. It may be no more than gossip, or jokes, or
exchanges of personal anecdote and incident, but it is still story:
narrative about people, telling what they did, how they did it,
and why. Literature in all its forms grew out of the oral tradition
and we cannot emphasize enough how deeply rooted in his early
oral experience is everyone's taste for reading. As for introducing
books to people during their childhood and adolescence, telling
stories and reading aloud are the two most effective methods, both
fundamental and essentially important. The reasons why are worth
isolating briefly before we come to the techniques involved.

To begin with, both methods are appetizers: they stimulate a
desire to read for oneself what one has heard told. This is especially
crucial at the time when children are learning the mechanics of
reading for themselves: the printed material they can cope with at
this stage is not only severely limited but too often lacks verbal and
imaginal richness, the kind of anaemia evident in that unhappy
'reading scheme' called 'Janet and John', among others. Through
listening to more satisfying language, from nursery rhymes and
tales to folk stories and such modern masterpieces as Sendak's
Where the Wild Things Are, children are kept in touch with the
pleasures that will come as soon as they have achieved a modicum
of mechanical skill. And later on, when their skills are well developed, the same methods lead them on, widening their reading
range, forming their taste, strengthening their capacity to comprehend complex language and to handle and appreciate increasingly
uncompromising literature. Without this stimulus many children
(and always those who need most help) will tend to settle down at a
very low level of proficiency, never reaching out beyond a minimal
satisfaction.

As children listen to stories, verse, prose of all kinds, they unconsciously become familiar with the rhythms and structures, the
cadences and conventions of the various forms of written language.
They are learning how print 'sounds', how to 'hear' it in their inner
ear. Only through listening to words in print being spoken does

anyone discover their colour, their life, their movement and drama. Most people, children as well as adults, 'read too much, too bittily and too quickly; they have no gears in their reading. Many of them make a thin response because they give little body – in terms of tone, manner, emotion, and so on – to their eye-reading; their inner ear is almost dead. They need to hear literature read well, and to practise reading it aloud.'* You can read satisfactorily for information without knowing about this, but you cannot appreciate and get full pleasure from literature without it. Story-telling and reading aloud are, therefore, more than good teaching methods by which to introduce books; they are essential, formative factors in everyone's literary education.

But another point must also be considered: the capacity of children to comprehend and enjoy language is frequently ahead of their ability to read. Most obviously this is true of those troubled with reading problems; but it is no less true, only less obvious, of most children, if not all, right up to adulthood (and through adulthood for some people). Listening to books read aloud bridges that gap, making available to children books they are mature enough to appreciate but which they cannot yet read with ease for themselves. Those with reading difficulties, of course, might never acquire enough skill; hearing books read will then be the *only* way they can receive the great body of the best literature in their native tongue.

Techniques common to both methods

In story-telling and reading aloud the principal instrument is the voice. An ugly voice, one that is monotonous or grating, weak in power, incomprehensible or strained, is never likely to receive and retain anyone's attention for long. On the other hand it is not necessary to have a superb actor's voice in order to succeed. Given practice, some careful thought, and perhaps a little training, every voice, except those physically defective, can be made serviceable; and certainly teachers who use their voices as tools of their trade should have no trouble in reaching a competent standard. Considering how necessary vocal control is to the profession, it seems to me very strange that student-teachers in most cases receive no guidance or help in their colleges on this subject, a state of affairs in need of reform.

The first thing to be learnt is how to listen to yourself. Unless you can hear what your voice is doing, you can never be sure it is doing what you want it to do. At first, as in playing the violin or riding a bike, the story-teller or reader is so busy concentrating on the mechanics of the business that he has no time to think about his

---

* Richard Hoggart, 'Teaching Literature to Adults' in *Speaking to Each Other*, Vol. Two, *About Literature*, Chatto and Windus, 1970, p. 220.

effect on other people. But after a while, when the mechanics have become second nature, he begins to refine his skill and can be both performer and listener at the same time. In getting this far a tape recorder is a great help and is afterwards a useful aid in rehearsing material to be told or read.

Very quickly, beginners discover the importance of breathing in voice control. Shallow breathing from the chest produces a thin sound that lacks resonance and energy as well as duration: breath comes, as the boy said, in short pants. Rather, the air should be brought from the diaphragm, so that the voice gains richness and power, and passages requiring long breaths can be sustained without loss of control. Practice is the only way to come by this facility, and texts like Shakespeare, the Authorized Version of the Bible, Milton, Wordsworth, Shaw and Eliot are the kind to work with because they make the biggest demands on depth of breathing as well as on the reader's skill in organizing the phrasing of the words.

It is little use, though, cultivating a well-controlled voice if what it says is incomprehensible. No one likes that artificial, over-precise articulation acquired by meticulously elocuted people who hang words on the air like so many ice-cubes. But lazy delivery, when the words are slurred and poorly shaped, or a thick accent difficult for people from outside the region to understand, are just as bad. It is quite possible to achieve clarity while preserving the personal and local flavour of your speech.

Breath control and clarity of articulation play major roles in projection, the ability to direct vocal sounds to the whole of an audience. This is not difficult to do in a confined space with only a few people present, but as soon as double figures are reached in the audience (as, for example, in a normal-sized class of children) in a room of more than domestic proportions attention must be paid to whether everyone present can hear comfortably. The instinct of un-skilled speakers is to add volume, to shout. That is a mistake. They may make themselves heard, but they also coarsen the quality of the sounds they produce, limiting the range and vocal colour. Projection is really a matter of energy rather than volume, and the energy comes from the diaphragm, which propels the breath like stones from a catapult so that the words are 'lobbed' from speaker to listeners. This is how actors on stage make themselves heard at the back of the auditorium even when speaking very quietly. Sup-porting the technique is an indefinable element: a consciousness of the audience and a desire to reach out to everyone in it, as though to touch them with sound. Projection also has to do with confidence. You have to want to communicate and feel capable of doing so. Self-effacing nervousness causes the epiglottis to tighten, strangling the words in the throat and stiffening the diaphragm so that it is like pulled-out elastic unable to propel anything. The story-teller has, in fact, to be something of a showman, a performer, before he gets anywhere.

Experience allied with self-criticism develops the art. But preparation – knowing what you are going to do and how you are going to do it – is indispensable to complete success. In preparing material the first thing to decide is the kind of vocal treatment each piece needs. Leacock's prototype goonery in *Soaked in Seaweed, or Upset in the Ocean*, one of the hilarious parodies included in *Nonsense Novels*, suits very well an exaggerated style of delivery, with caricatured voices in the dialogue, mock-heroic narrator, and moments of fast-paced farcical melodrama, yet all performed with total seriousness and belief. As the actor said, never play farce as though it were funny. Folk tales, on the other hand, benefit usually from the conversational manner, the round-the-fireside tale told nevertheless with careful attention paid to rhythm and phrasing, pace and subtlety of vocal tone: a very different approach to the Leacock ebullience. Sendak's *Where the Wild Things Are*, when read aloud to young children as they look at the unrivalled pictures, needs a firm, quiet voice, until that glorious wordless pictorial passage showing the 'wild rumpus', when at least one reader has discovered it is necessary 'to perform like a one-man band while the pictures are being absorbed and [I] have found that my own grotesque variations on the galumphing passage from the Great C Major fit the case admirably.'*

Of course, in reading aloud the words are supplied by a text; in story-telling (unless a text has been memorized, which is one way of going about it, as we shall see) the words are the performer's, and this adds another crucial preparatory problem. Just as delivery must be tuned to suit the kind of material chosen, so must the language used to tell a story. It is, naturally, difficult to demonstrate this in print. But there are written stories which show something of the kind of thing I mean. Take, for example, this Westmorland version of a jocular folk tale:

> There's some as thinks a farm lad must have a good memory, and there's a tale about it. A farmer had just hired a lad, and he wanted to make sure he had a good memory. Well, in the evening, about nine o'clock, they's been settin' afore t' fire, an' he reckoned he'd try t'lad. 'Well,' he said tull 'un, 'it's time we was going to t' *Easy Decree*.' 'What's *Easy Decree*?' asked t'lad. 'Bed's *Easy Decree*,' said t' farmer, 'we've lots of odd names for different maks of things here; I ca' my breeches *Forty Frappers*.' 'Oh!' says t'lad, 'an' what d'ye call the stairs?' '*L.K.C.*'
>
> Then t'lad sees t'cat. 'And what d'ye call t' cat?' 'That's *Grey-*

*Brian Alderson, 'Bodley Head Wild Things on the Horizon', *Children's Book News*, Vol. 2 No. 2, 1967, p. 54.

Faced Jeffer.' 'And what d'ye call t'fire?' '*Popolorum.*' 'And yer well?' '*Resolution.*' 'And yer hay-mew?' '*Mount Etna*, that's as good a name as I can come by. And now we'll away to this *Easy Decree*, but think on ye say them words ower to yoursel' till you're perfectly sure on 'em.'

Well, next morning, t'lad was up early to put t'fire on. He warn't just looking, and t'fire spread to t'cat's tail, that was just settin' by, and so t'cat felt its tail swinged, and ran out of t'kitchen, towards t'barn. And t'lad, as soon as he saw what was happening, up and shouted: 'Now, *Maister, Maister*, come rise from thy *Easy Decree*, put on thy *Forty Frappers*, and come down *L.K.C.* for the *Grey-Faced Jeffer* has gitten *Popolorum* to his tail, and he's off to *Mount Etna*, without *Resolution*, and all will be burned.' 'Aye,' says t'farmer, 'thou's aw reet, lad. Thou's gitten a good memory.' (1. Pt. A vol. 2 p. 66)

Collected in 1907 from an oral source, this story depends for its charm and attraction on the colloquial flavour, its dialect, and would lose a lot by being formalized and standardized. A reader who cannot inflect the words as they ought to be should not attempt to perform the piece.

Contrast this with the adaptation of 'Yallery Brow' by Alan Garner (he calls the story 'the most powerful of all English fairy tales' and one is inclined to agree). Garner retains the folk quality, avoiding 'the obscurities of dialect without losing the vivid language'. He thereby creates a version many tellers can manage who have no command of the original Lincolnshire. Here is a snatch of Garner's version:

I was in a fine rage, and should liked to have kicked him, but it was no good, there wasn't enough of him to get my boot against.

But I said to once: 'Look here, master, I'll thank you to leave me alone after this, do you hear? I want none of your help, and I'll have nowt more to do with you – see now.'

The horrid thing brak out with a screeching laugh, and pointed his brown finger at me.

'Ho ho, Tom!' says he. 'You've thanked me, my lad, and I told you not, I told you not!'

'I don't want your help, I tell you!' I yelled at him. 'I only want never to see you again, and to have nowt more to do with you. You can go!'

The thing only laughed and screeched and mocked, as long as I went on swearing . . . (2. p. 49).

This is brilliant editorial work, because it leaves the original qualities untouched, and provides a perfect example of how the storyteller should handle folk material in preparing it for himself. The whole question of the language used in folk stories and the qualities to look for is studied at length by Elizabeth Cook in *The Ordinary and the Fabulous* (3), a book of inexhaustible value to teachers and all those engaged in story-telling and reading aloud. I hope I have said enough here to stress the importance of linguistic style and to indicate that for the beginner an urgent task is that he discover the styles most natural to him. Once he has a few pieces at his command, widening his collection is an easier task: he can experiment without anxiety because at each trial the new material can be supported by the old so that his confidence is not undermined if it fails. What ought certainly to be avoided is reliance on the same stock of material, the same stock linguistically or in theme and content. One must be ever open to fresh ideas, new possibilities, always on the look-out for suitable additions to the repertoire.

Preparation for a story-teller is like rehearsal for an orchestra: the score is explored for its shape, its structure. There will be passages that need emphasis, and some that need a slow pace, others that need a quickened tempo, and so on. Central to this process is the pause. In the age of Harold Pinter and Peter Brook we ought all to have learnt the part pause plays in the drama of spoken language. Like sounds, pauses have different lengths, different intensities, can be emphasized or ignored. They frame words, form them into significant phrases, can even alter meaning, and infuse emotion. It is when speakers have no feeling for pause that their speech seems to burble on without any arresting quality. The club bore is a burbler: he has not learnt the eloquence of silence.

Basically, pauses are necessary to meaning. Look at these lines from Act Two, Scene Two of *Macbeth*:

> No; this my hand will rather
> The multitudinous seas incarnadine,
> Making the green one red.

The usual interpretation given is to pause after 'No', then again after 'incarnadine', and then in the last line to touch lightly on 'the' and put an equal emphasis on 'green one red'. The first two pauses are straightforward enough; change them or omit them and the meaning becomes confused, or at least difficult to follow. But the last line is troublesome. Some actors, in order to try and help the meaning, pause slightly after 'green one', and this is unobjectionable. Michael Horden, however, in a performance some years back, chose to pause after 'green', giving the phrase as:

> Making the green . . . one red.

The effect was unusual, but it was somehow also a shade comic, which was not at all the intention.

Meaning aside, pauses are used to mould dramatic shape. Here is a passage from Philippa Pearce's novel for children, *A Dog So Small*, which demonstrates my point:

'Open it, Ben,' said his mother; and his father reminded him, 'Use your new knife on the string, boy.' Ben never noticed the sharpness of the Sheffield steel as he cut the string round the parcel and then un-folded the wrapping-paper.

They had sent him a picture instead of a dog.

And then he realized that they *had* sent him a dog, after all. He almost hated them for it. His dog was worked in woollen cross stitch, and framed and glazed as a little picture.*

Ben is expecting, with the kind of longing children feel deeply, a present of a dog from his grandparents for his birthday. In the brilliantly created breakfast-time scene (chapter two) from which my extract is taken, a scene underplayed, superficially calm, sparely but precisely detailed, and trembling with the boy's tension under all, Ben realizes that he is not to have his promised gift. It is a moment when he feels betrayed by two people of whom he is very fond. The scene is so elegantly presented on the page that whether reading aloud or silently the drama is almost visible in the lay-out of the words, until the climactic moment, pin-pointed by that one-sentence paragraph: 'They had sent him a picture instead of a dog.'

The unskilled reader will blunder through, without separating the sentence from the paragraphs before and after by pauses of the right dramatic weight. No very great shift in the tonal quality of the voice is needed: a slower, firmer delivery of the line perhaps, but nothing exaggerated, no drum-roll treatment. The quiet statement of fact fits better; the pauses do all the work.

Not all writers are so consummately clever in constructing their work as Philippa Pearce, however, and when they are not, the reader has to sort out for himself what qualities of sound and pause to give, without looking for author guidance. This means that several interpretations might have to be tried both in rehearsal and in performance before a definitive version is found which retains the integrity of the text and also suits the reader. For story-telling and reading aloud are performance arts: they involve a script (even when the words are improvised on the spot), an interpreter (the teller or reader), and an audience, and as in all performances, the audience plays a part in moulding the finished work.

Most authorities rightly warn us, however, that telling and reading are not the same as acting. A story-teller is 'spinning a yarn', 'weaving a tale' with words as his material – the old images suggest the anecdotal, conversational quality that must be striven for. An actor, on the other hand, works through movement quite as much as through words, and frequently has to suggest a character

* Philippa Pearce, *A Dog So Small*, Longman Young Books, 1962, Puffin Books, 1964, p. 16. The whole chapter is worth studying from the point of view of dramatic quality.

different from himself. The story-teller relies on his own personality: he tells the tale, does not assume in himself the characters in the tale. This is why actors often are poor readers: they want to 'play' not 'tell'. The Longman Imprint Series of books also includes some recordings to accompany anthologies of stories. On one disc Stan Barstow reads some of his own work. What we get is Barstow speaking his words in his own voice: the style is quiet, intimate, personal, undemonstrative, and exactly suited to his writing. The characters in the stories are hinted at vocally, but not impersonated. It is just like a man telling his friends about an incident that happened to him; it is moving and wholly convincing without being theatrical. On another disc John Neville reads stories by Sid Chaplin. Here we get the studied, acted rendering: the narrator has his own voice, impeccably standard English; the characters are 'played' – and in the wrong dialect for Chaplin. For sure, Neville underplays, isn't at all 'hammy', and his phrasing is carefully judged, his sympathy with the text sincere. But he is, nevertheless, a one-man theatre company, not a reader, and the result is far less effective though it may well be professionally more accomplished than Barstow's. What is missing is the intimate, easy tone: the sense of a single personality.

Of course, it is dangerous to generalize, because I am not suggesting that there is but one way to read and tell stories – that characters should never have their own voices and that one should always just 'talk' the words. I have indeed emphasized that each piece will require its own style. But they must be styles that fit the performer. Dylan Thomas is an interesting example from this point of view. His natural vocal manner was declamatory and sonorous. He pronounced his poetry (as Hopkins also asked that his should be said) and his marvellous tumbling prose like an inspired orator, which he was. But he could adjust that full-bodied, hall-filling, resonant instrument to fit the demands of a radio microphone without losing a note of the fullness, and that ability made his one of the most compelling radio voices I have ever heard. Thomas was a great verbal performer, but he was never an actor; what you got was Dylan Thomas, *his* language and *his* personality. With timing precise and neat, phrasing skilled and controlled, he designed everything for dramatic effect, and even in his last days when he puffed audibly his breathing still supported his voice and gave it energy. A master of the art, it is death to imitate him, as it is always dangerous to imitate other people. One can learn from the techniques of the great performers and so improve one's own work, but imitation becomes first parody and at last a gutless façade empty of the one thing that matters: a living, voice-carried personality that is one's own.

Story-telling

The most commonplace, direct source of story-telling material is personal incident, the kind of thing that in ordinary conversation might be introduced with a phrase like, 'You'll never guess what's just happened to me. . . .' Every teacher, I suppose, has his own collection of favourite yarns based on this autobiographical starting point. The usefulness of such an approach is obvious: it very quickly establishes the right tone in the relationship between teacher-storyteller and the children-audience. And because the teller is sharing something of himself, the children in their turn respond by wanting to share something of themselves in the same way. This is itself important for they are thus engaged in using language creatively, a preparatory experience that helps them to reach an understanding of what literature is all about.

This is, however, only a starting point, a kind of literary gossip. One also needs a large collection of stories, which will be drawn mostly from printed sources even though one tells them 'spontaneously' each time, using no script. There are different ways of handling these.

One method is to learn the story by heart as an actor learns his lines. Some stories, Beatrix Potter's for example, are so written that the exact form of the words, the exact words used in fact, are essential to the tale. And some stories are so well known, or become so well known to children because they enjoy hearing them again and again, that a cry of protest goes up if the words are changed at all. Material of this nature must be committed to memory – or, at least, the essentially unalterable parts must be – otherwise it is best to read aloud rather than story-tell. The method has one big disadvantage: rote-learned material can go stale after a few performances, just as a play can go stale for actors. It is often better therefore to begin by reading a story, either to oneself or to children until the ingredients are familiar – the narrative shape, the plot, the characters, the details of time, place, motive, atmosphere, theme, moments of climax and suspense – and then to tell the story on future occasions in one's own words. The performance is kept fresh each time because the teller is under a tension: he has to find the language in which to clothe the body of the work.

The great American story-teller, Frances Clarke Sayers, having advised the beginner to 'steep himself in folklore until the elemental themes, the folk wisdom, the simplicity of characterization, the universality of their attitudes, are part of himself',* explains how best to get command of a tale:

* Frances Clarke Sayers, 'The Storyteller's Art' in *Summoned by Books*, The Viking Press, New York, 1965, p. 100.

After you have chosen a story you long to tell, read it over and over and then analyse it. What in it has appealed to you? The humour?, The ingenuity of the plot? What is its mood? And when you have isolated mood and appeal, consciously, this too will colour the telling of the story.

Where is the climax? Make a note of it in your mind, so that you can indicate to the children by pause, by quickening of the pace, the peak of the tale. Then read it again, and over and over. Then see if you can list, or call over in your mind, the order of the events of the story, the hinges of action, in their correct sequence. With these fully in mind, read the tale again, this time for turns of phrase you may want to remember. When these have been incorporated into your story, tell it to yourself, silently, just before you go to sleep at night, or while riding a bus or subway. After all this, you will find that the story is yours forever. For though you may forget it, after years of neglect, one reading of it will restore it to you, once you have mastered it thoroughly.

Do not memorize a story, unless it is a story by Kipling, Sandburg, or Walter de la Mare, for the great stylists must be memorized, especially when they use language in ways of their own. Half the joy of the *Just So Stories* would be lost if they were told in any language other than that in which Kipling wrote them. Even when a story is memorized, it is well to have gained control of it in the manner which has been here indicated.*

The best material to use in this approach is that great corpus of traditional folk and fairy tale, myth, legend, and stories from Biblical and historical sources. These have particular appeal to children and are especially suited to being told for reasons which Elizabeth Cook has already summed up better than I can in some comments she makes about fairy tales becoming the peculiar property of the nursery only by historical accident:

Nevertheless the accidents that gave these stories to children were happy ones. Children under eleven are eager to know what happens next, and impatient with anything that stops them from getting on with the story. They want to listen to conversations only if direct speech is the quickest and clearest method of showing what was transacted between two people as a necessary preliminary to what these two people proceeded to *do*. At about nine or ten they are beginning to be interested in character, but in a very straightforward and moral way: they see people as marked by one particular attribute, cleverness, or kindness, or strictness, or being a good shot, and they mind whether things are right or wrong. They are especially sensitive to the heroic virtue of justice, and they are beginning to notice why people are tempted to be unjust. They are not interested in the long processes of inner debate by which people make difficult decisions, and become very irritated with grown-ups who insist upon giving them not only the practical answer or information they asked for, but also

* Ibid., pp. 104–105.

all the reasons for it. They expect a story to be a good yarn, in which the action is swift and the characters are clearly and simply defined. And legends and fairy tales are just like that. Playground games show that children like catastrophes and exhibitions of speed and power, and a clear differentiation between cowboys, cops and spacemen who are good, and Indians, robbers and space monsters who are bad.

Magic has a particular attraction for eight-to-ten-year-olds, but not because it is pretty or 'innocent'. They delight, in more senses than the usual one, in seeing how far they can go. If some people are taller than others, how tall could anyone conceivably be? If some people are cleverer than others at making things, could someone alter what things are actually made of? If there are different languages which different people understand, could there be a secret language that affected things and people against their will? Such speculations carried *ad infinitum* are given concrete form in giants, and the enchantments of elves and dwarfs, and the magic of runes and spells. (3. p. 7)

One could not better describe criteria for selecting stories for telling and reading to children before adolescence than Elizabeth Cook does here. And she goes on to point out a subsidiary quality in this kind of material which is worth remembering:

Stories that lead to doing things are all the more attractive to children, who are active rather than passive creatures. Myths and fairy tales provide an unusually abundant choice of things to do. Largely because they are archetypal and anonymous (in quality, if not in provenance), they will stand reinterpretation in many forms without losing their character. They can be recreated by children not only in words but in drama, in mime, in dance and in painting. Action in them is not fussy, and lends itself to qualitative expression in the movements of the human body and in the shapes and colours of non-figurative painting. (3. p. 9)

In summary: story-telling is in many ways far more demanding as an art than reading aloud; more demanding in linguistic and technical skills, more demanding in preparation. It is, however, an art of great power and educative value, worth all the effort and time it takes to learn and perfect.

Reading aloud

If story-telling is more demanding on the performer, reading aloud is more demanding on the listener. To begin with, it is a less conversational art, less of a direct communication between teller and listener: there is a physical object, the book-source, in between. But of greater importance than this is the fact that written words are frequently more compacted in meaning, more sophisticated in constructions than language used in the spontaneous form of story-telling. So the listener requires more time to receive the meaning, to take in what is happening. He is helped in this if he can see the reader clearly, is close enough to watch the facial expressions which hint at the drama of the text and to feel the personality of the performer. Furthermore:

> If the reading remains no more than spoken print, if it fails to bring the print off the page and convert it into people and events, thought and feeling, it will do more harm than good. Reading out loud can be an oppressive exercise for all involved. The reader should see what he is reading about vividly in his imagination, for what he is sharing with the listener is something that is alive in him. It is not easy to maintain an imaginative reading. The concentration of an inexperienced reader can flag by the end of the first paragraph and he can quickly lose awareness of his audience; the reading becomes mechanical, without meaning, so the reader has to make a conscious effort to rededicate himself to the performance from time to time. (4. p. 120)

Younger children, before and after the time they learn to read, like to look at the book as well as at the reader while they listen. Older children feel that compulsion less forcefully. But there are times when it is right that they should have copies of the text in which they can follow the reading if they wish. This is obviously so if we are reading a text in which the language is very much more difficult than the children can yet read for themselves. Seeing the words helps them to understand what they are hearing and links sound and sight of new words so that their vocabulary is stretched by a look–hear, as well as a look–say method. There are also times when we want children to attend more closely to a piece of writing than they can by hearing only. Having read a story or poem through once we may want to re-read it, pausing here and there to dwell on a passage, to savour it and talk about it. Unless everyone involved can refer back to the text this cannot be done with complete success; usually it means the teacher is the only person who says anything. One might almost formulate a principle that the deeper we want to engage the listener in a *conscious* recognition of many different aspects and qualities of literature the more necessary it becomes for him to follow the reading in a text. If we look again at the extract from *A Dog So Small* quoted on page 49 it is possible to demonstrate what I mean.

The whole of the chapter that includes the extract might well be read aloud as an introduction to the book, and children can easily enjoy the drama of Ben's situation, its truth-to-life quality as well as its taut atmosphere. But suppose we want them to see the nuances of the writing: the way the different members of the family treat the boy's predicament, perhaps, or Ben's carefully suggested bitterness and anger. Unless everyone has a copy to look at, it will be hard for them to pick out exactly the words that create these aspects of the story. They will have felt but not necessarily remembered the precise references that, put together, build up the picture.

Tucked away, for example, in the paragraph beginning 'And then he realized that they *had* sent him a dog . . .' is one short but staggering sentence which exactly states how Ben felt about his grandparents for breaking their promise. 'He almost hated them for it.' But because this comes so quickly after the one-sentence paragraph that marks the climactic moment in this part of the scene, the revelation of Ben's feelings can be passed over without being noticed, even though it has its effect. When the chapter is finished and children talk about it, they might agree that Ben was 'mad', 'annoyed' or 'upset', but they baulk often at the idea that he 'almost hated' his grandparents. Hating grandparents is an uncomfortable idea for children. Ask them to look back through the chapter to see if we have been told exactly how Ben felt and they come across that glowering statement, 'He almost hated them for it', at which some express surprise, some critical disbelief, and some show pleasure at having textually confirmed what they thought they knew but could not prove without evidence. It is a moment when the profound and subtle undercurrents that play beneath the surface of this deceptively simple book suddenly reveal themselves, or, to change the metaphor, it is like finding one piece in a jigsaw puzzle that helps you place many others.

If we want to lead children gradually to an awareness of the qualities in literature, this is how we can do it best: by reading to them from rich texts and providing opportunities afterwards for response tested against the written words. This is not a matter of cold analysis, against which I warned earlier, but rather of finding patterns: patterns of plot and character and words. As Elizabeth Cook remarks in the book already cited, children 'are often fascinated by consistency for its own sake, liking patterns because they are patterns'. And let me hurriedly stress yet again that I do not mean we should be constantly stopping in mid-stream during a reading to ask questions and provoke discussion. Patterns can only be discovered when we see things as a whole. George Sampson has some pertinent comments about this:

> What we must not do, and what I fear we often do, is to mix two different kinds of lesson. We must not turn the reading of a play or a poem into a study of form or language, or we shall be trying to live on two planes at once. The explicatory lesson is one thing, and the presentation of a poem something quite different. What pleasure should we get from a performance of the C minor Symphony if the conductor stopped the orchestra at every occurrence of the main theme to expatiate upon the wonderful significance with which Beethoven can invest a simple rhythmic phrase? . . . It is delightful to have these beauties of musical language pointed out to us; but not while we are

on the emotional plane of a performance. If explanation and performance are put together we get good from neither; but isn't our usual method of dealing with school literature rather like a blend of explanation and performance? It needs must be that explanations come: but woe unto those that foist them into the very utterance of poetry!*

These are some of the ways we can handle reading performances:

1. A whole short story read at a sitting. Nothing at all might be said afterwards, or discussion may occur spontaneously immediately the reading is over or in a later lesson. After the discussion everyone may feel they would like to hear the story again the better to appreciate it in the light of what has been said.

2. A 'programme' of short stories, poems, prose passages might be put together and read as a spoken anthology. Between each piece there should be a brief interlude or linking passage, and discussion may flow during these interludes or after the programme is over. An example of children using this idea is given on page 62.

3. One part of a novel or long text may be read in order to whet the listeners' appetites for reading the book themselves. The part chosen should have a unity of its own, a wholeness that offers a complete experience without at the same time giving away everything. I have quoted chapter two of *A Dog So Small* because it has this quality: it is a complete scene, needs little prior explanation and preparation for the audience to understand what is going on, ends on a high note, an emotional and narrative climax, and leaves a question mark hanging in the air to lead listeners on: what happens next?

4. Serializations that can be contained within a few sessions, one following another in quick succession, say, all in one week. *The Boy Who Was Afraid* by Armstrong Sperry provides a perfect example of this. The book is short – 92 generously printed pages, including eight and a half pages of illustrations, chapters ending on a few lines of print and the story beginning on page seven of the text. Much enjoyed by late primary and early secondary-school aged children, the story is in five chapters, each dealing with a self-contained part of the plot. These five parts can each be read in about 35 to 40 minutes: just about enough time for children of this age to be asked to listen. Thus in five lessons, one a day, the book can be performed serially in a week. It is the kind of narrative which draws out discussion from children, but after it is finished, when its neatly constructed plot and folk-tale-like treatment can be fully appreciated.

5. Serializations spread over five or six weeks, a little being read each day. This is a traditional method – I remember a number of books being read to me like this, though none with more pleasure

* George Sampson, *English for the English*, pp. 94–95.

than *Heidi* at the age of ten and *Treasure Island* a year later. For all but upper secondary-aged pupils, it is unwise to spread serialization over longer than six weeks – half a term – and even this is too long for junior primary-school children. The time span is determined by the audience's ability to keep in mind as the reading progresses all the major elements (details which have plot significance, for instance, and the relationships between characters); once these details become confused or vague in the memory interest and enjoyment are soon lost and boredom sets in. Of course, this has to do not only with the total length of time the serialization takes but the time that elapses between readings, a period that should never exceed one week. Even then each session should begin with a brief recap of the previous week's reading and 'the story so far'.

Reading time has another dimension that needs attention: the time of each session. Obviously, the younger the child the less he can take. Infant children may be satisfied by a few minutes of listening; by the age of ten, twenty to thirty minutes should be about right for all but 'backward' children; and by the end of secondary school, forty minutes to an hour is bearable, though at every stage readings should be treated like play or music performances: there should be 'acts' or 'movements' with brief intervals between for relaxing the concentration and the body. Intervals do not have to be filled with talk, either. They can be simply 'breathing spaces'. But always, in every aspect of this kind of teaching, two factors guide us, indicating what to do: the nature of the material being read and the response of the listeners. A difficult book takes more concentrated attention than something much easier, and this will alter the length of time children can attend to it. Some books provoke vocal responses – a kind of literary effervescent effect – while others seem to turn people in on themselves, when they prefer to say nothing but savour the reading in silence. I have found, for example, in reading extracts from Scott's diary of his trip to the South Pole that fourteen-year-olds interrupted all the time to ask questions and make observations, until the final entries were reached, when everyone went very quiet, moved deeply by Scott's words and unwilling to bruise the emotion they felt. On the whole, the stronger the emotional power of writing the less children want to say about it. And this, to my mind, is something to be respected. If we have selected well and prepared our readings beforehand, then we can afford to relax during 'performance': we can give ourselves up to the words, enjoying them as much as we hope the children do, and allowing the session to control itself, to follow its own path, because whatever happens there will be a feeling of rightness about it, of mutual sharing and participation and pleasure. Whether we speak or listen, pause or go on, break off sooner than expected or continue longer than normally, these things will sort themselves out according to the way a number of factors interact on each occasion, factors such as the quality of our performance, the kind of text being read, the receptivity and mood of the audience, the whole set and setting of the event. The best teachers seem to introduce reading aloud and story-telling into their work with spontaneous ease without at the same time losing any of the sense of drama and specialness, and their children settle down to listen with an unfussy expectation of pleasure to come. The whole business has an air of familiarity because it happens every day, yet it has a freshness and excitement too, because there is always something new and enjoyable to be shared. But for a teacher to get himself and his pupils this far requires thought and skill and a genuine belief in, as well as wide knowledge of, all literature. 'All of this' wrote Frances Clarke Sayers in summary of the story-teller's art that applies as a summary of everything said here, 'demands a great investment of time. Yet there is hardly any other investment, hardly any other area of study, that yields so potent a means of making literature live for children.'*

Children as tellers and readers

An old teacher of mine, a cynical little fellow of no great professional ability, used to tell us that teachers were nothing else but broken-down actors who liked the sound of their own voices. We would laugh and mutter that in his case the cap fitted. But he had a point. It is very easy to fall into the trap of enjoying the act of telling stories and reading aloud so much that the children never get a chance. Especially when they are happy enough to sit and listen as long as their teacher likes because he does it so well. A balance is important: children have their part to play in telling and reading.

I have already said that on the whole it is not difficult to stimulate children into telling stories; beginning with personal anecdotes they can soon be led to invent and embroider imaginatively. And they succeed with oral narrative more easily and satisfyingly than with written stories: they are not so inhibited by all the mechanical and technical problems like spelling, sentence structure, the distractingly slow speed of handwriting that frustrates excitement and coherence and head-long flow of language. Writing is often a chore; telling stories is an uncluttered pleasure. Certainly if children are to write with any real success and understanding of what they are doing it is a necessary part of their apprenticeship that they first feel their way into the art through the experience gained from seeing the effect of their stories on an audience. Even then the

* Frances Clarke Sayers, 'The Storyteller's Art', p. 106.

business of setting children exercises in story writing – the old fashioned 'composition' – is suspect. In a very useful chapter on this subject in *Children and Fiction* E. W. Hildick points out the weakness:

> As a professional author, with years of experience behind me, I know only too well how difficult it is to work to a schedule, even when the units are days – so much work per day. With authors, this reluctance to sit down to write is often not so much a matter of laziness as of a fear that as soon as they pick up their pens or strike the keys of their typewriters they will begin to distort the concepts and images they wish to convey. Thus this starting difficulty exists even when the incentive and inspiration and ideas are there. How unutterably unreasonable it is, therefore, to expect children to sit down and write, or continue to write, stories during firmly fixed half-hour or forty-five-minute periods. How unutterably unreasonable it is indeed to expect them to sit down and remain sitting down at all during such an activity, when grown men and women whose very business it is to write fiction need so often to do other things as part of the process: to pace about, for example; or stand up at a high desk; or play records; or stare out of the window; or lie flat on their backs; or drink three stiff very dry martinis in quick succession; or shout at the cat; or make love to their secretaries; or pick their noses. . . . Especially unutterably unreasonable is this when the children in question haven't the vocabularies, the simple prose technique or sometimes even the basic physical handwriting skills to keep pace with their imaginations, which are so inclined to run away with them when they *are* inspired and ready to go. (5. p. 155)

Oral story-making can spring off from things that happen in the local community: robberies, the arrival of strangers, the building of a new estate and the preparatory demolition work, street accidents, big sports events, a strike: any detail that suggests a crisis of one kind or another into which people, with their strengths and weaknesses emphasized, will be drawn. The local newspaper offers plenty of clues, and children themselves contribute others. From this beginning plots can be developed by children either in groups or as a class, characters can be invented or elaborated from real people. This is the approach Hildick uses in his Storypacks, collections of documentary material about fictional people and their environments.(6) What he is doing, what we as teachers should be doing, is helping children to bring together the raw material every author needs before he can put flesh and bone onto a basic idea: maps and charts, photographs and settings taken from life, outline facts about characters – their physical appearances, prejudices, tastes, attitudes, beliefs, opinions, idiosyncrasies. As the basic raw material accumulates, questions are asked. How would this character behave in this situation? What would X do if Y did this, given all the circumstances we know about them? At this stage it is not the finished story that matters but rather the imaginative exploration of people and the possibilities of action open to them. The effect is two-fold: the children's imaginative powers are exercised and developed; and – the important point in this context – their appreciation of the processes and function of literature is deepened. Because they have worked as an author works they are better equipped to see what can be done with words used imaginatively, and, hopefully, will begin to look at what they read with more searching eyes.

This kind of invention – collecting raw material and fitting it into an imaginative structure – is not something that relies on inspiration or talent or an inventive mind. It can be done at any time by any group of children capable of reading and talking about a given theme for half an hour or so at a time. We are not seeking polished works of art nor brilliant performances: it is the act of creation that matters and from which the benefits of this method flow. We are concerned with what Hildick calls 'the logistics involved in the creation of fiction: the preparation of the elements, the components, the details of character and background and situation that most professionals have to deal with consciously or unconsciously, whether in elaborate notes or in jottings on the backs of old envelopes, before they embark on the actual writing of the story.' (5. p. 161)

Other methods put to work alongside this shift the emphasis from the creative process to telling stories to each other. These stories may depend on narratives invented by the children if they opt for this (but not otherwise) or on sources which provide the stories whole and which the children can tell in their own way, adapting as they wish. I'm not thinking only of specially written children's stories, but of a wide range of material. Every locality, for instance, has its corpus of folk lore which children can discover for themselves in preparation for story-telling sessions devoted to it. I was brought up in County Durham very near the setting of The Lambton Worme, a version of which appears in Joseph Jacobs' *English Fairy Tales*. I first heard the story from my grandfather and it has fascinated me ever since. Yet I do not remember any teacher making use of it in my infant or primary schools, something that seems to me now a strange neglect. This local tale could have been used to set me and my class-mates off on a search for the other worme stories that litter the area up and down the east coast of Britain. We'd have found The Laidly Worme of Spindleston Heugh, The Pollard Worme, The Helstone Worme, The Linton Worme, and many others. Discovering these tales, looking out printed versions and comparing them with the oral tradition would have introduced us step by step into the rich lode of folk lore, and from there we could have been led on to read the adaptations from folk lore in the work of writers like Rosemary Sutcliff, Ian Serraillier, Barbara Leonie Picard and many more, and so at last to the core books: the Norse Sagas, *The Iliad* and *The Odyssey*, and so on. Story-telling is for children, as it was for the human race, a participatory art from which is born a literary consciousness which by adulthood has grown into a full-bodied appreciation of the work of the great imaginative writers.

Reading aloud needs a great deal of careful handling when children are the performers. If selection of material is important for an adult reader of skill and experience, how much more important it is for children. And if preparation is indispensable to an adult, how can it be otherwise for a child? Yet we go on asking children to read from sight anything we happen to think they ought to be able to manage, regardless of such simple principles. We still behave as though we thought that once a child can decipher individual words, we have taught him to read, when, in fact, we have done no such thing. The unit of reading either silently or aloud is not the single word but the phrase, and the unit of complete expression in print is not so much the sentence as the paragraph. There is a lot of work to be done with children after they have learnt to recognize printed words.

By now it should hardly be necessary to condemn the practice of 'reading round the class'. Nothing is more deadening, tortuous, and degrading to children as readers as well as to the words they are allowed to garble. Yet it is still a method imposed in some schools: the lazy teacher's refuge from hard work, thoughtful planning and organization, and patience. Reading round the class is essentially so wrong because it is a method that mixes up different purposes that ought never to be mixed. If we want children to listen to something read with enjoyment and for the sake of what is read then we cannot at the same time hope to practise their ability to read aloud well. And if we want to give reading practice then we should see that not only do the children understand what is happening but also that as few of them have to endure the others' difficulties as possible. A musician practises his instrument and his music privately, he does not do it during a concert, at which he performs a finished, rehearsed score as perfectly as he can. The same working rules should apply to children and their reading aloud. Basically, therefore, there are three main kinds of lesson.

1. PRACTICE
These are sessions when the techniques of reading aloud are taught not for their own sake, but as part of the preparations, the 'rehearsals', for a 'performance'. The texts chosen should be suited to the particular aspect we wish to concentrate on at each time: phrasing, articulation, breathing, dealing with unfamiliar words.

It is not necessary to hold such lessons in large groups. The children can be split up into ones or twos, or small groups of four or five, depending on the nature of the work in hand. Tape recorders can be put to work, individual children using them to listen to themselves and their reading. There can be plenty of instruction and criticism between teacher and taught and between children within their groups. At the outset each time, the children are told clearly what is being asked of them and what is being looked for – what aspect of the work is to be concentrated on. And never is the activity sullied and warped by competition between children to see whether one can read 'better' than another. Nor are these training periods held in a purposeless vacuum: they are like the musician's work on scales and fingering and fundamental techniques, the groundwork on which is built the ability to perform for other people's enjoyment. There is always eventually a goal: a time when the art is to be used.

2. PREPARATION (OR REHEARSAL)

These lessons follow on from the above and are concerned with specific texts which are to be read aloud. The actor is preparing his lines, so to speak. Let us suppose that a group of ten-year-olds of mixed ability are preparing a 'programme' of readings about cats. They have chosen, with the teacher's help, a collection including a few poems, a reading of Kipling's *The Cat Who Walked by Himself*, and a dramatized reading of the Cheshire Cat passage from *Alice in Wonderland*. All the children involved will work together. Having read through their allotted material silently until they are familiar with it, they begin to read aloud to each other, listening to criticisms and suggestions about how their performance might be improved. The teacher, who may well be dealing with two or three other groups at the same time, will join in from time to time to guide, correct, and help. When the material was being shared out he will have made sure that every member of the group got something that was within his reading capabilities after a certain amount of practice. The Kipling story, as the longest and probably the most difficult piece, will be in the hands of the most developed performer; any children with reading problems will have something very much less demanding but which can at the same time be enjoyed for its own sake: a short poem, perhaps, or a few words after each piece, linking the one with the next. Part of the group's task will be to dramatize the Cheshire Cat sequence, and to prepare scripts for it, which may end up as a play-reading for three voices:

NARRATOR: Alice was a little startled by seeing the Cheshire Cat sitting on a bough of a tree a few yards off. The cat only grinned when it saw her.

ALICE: It looks good natured.

NARRATOR: She thought. Still – it had very long claws and a great many teeth, so she felt that it ought to be treated with respect.

ALICE: Cheshire Puss.

NARRATOR: She began, rather timidly, as she did not know whether it would like the name: however, it only grinned a little wider.

ALICE: Come, it's pleased so far.

NARRATOR: Thought Alice, and she said:

ALICE: Would you tell me, please, which way I ought to go from here?

CAT: That depends a good deal on where you want to get to.

ALICE: I don't much care where –

And so on. When the children are working individually instead of in groups they can be put together in pairs to help each other.

3. THE READING PERFORMANCE

Everything said about a teacher reading aloud, and about set and setting for the activity, applies here. The primary aim is that whatever is read should be enjoyed. I have suggested the idea of 'programmes' done by groups of children, but there are other ideas worth using:

(i) 'Your story time' – a period set aside for one pupil to read his own selection of prose or verse. These sessions may be only a few minutes long or take up a whole lesson, depending on the child's age and ability. He will know well in advance when he is to perform and will have selected his material and rehearsed with the aid of his teacher. Children who are upset by an 'audience' or who cannot sustain their reading for very long might be helped by recording their performance: this can be done over a number of days, their reading being taped in short passages which can be prepared and then recorded as often as necessary until they manage a satisfactory version. This same technique can, of course, be elaborated upon and used to create items similar to radio programmes for playing to other classes or groups. It has the added advantage that the children involved hear their own work, when they tend to be much more self-critical than they are without such an aid.

(ii) Dramatized readings, when a story or poem is prepared on the lines demonstrated in the Cheshire Cat passage above, are entertaining and also involve children in a number of worthwhile procedures. They must, for example, prepare the script, which necessitates discussion of the text and how properly to interpret it, a basically critical exercise of a valuable kind. Because each child has only one bit to read, he can concentrate on the vocal presentation of that single part without having to worry about all the other different parts as he would have to if he were reading the entire piece. This also means that children of varying abilities can work together, for among the single parts there will usually be some of slight difficulty and short length.

Of course, not all material can be treated like this. The most suitable includes plenty of dialogue, or, at any rate, opportunities for different voices to add something by way of variety and texture as well as enhanced meaning. Undoubtedly this kind of choral adaptation of prose and verse when well prepared and presented is attractive and entertaining to listen to and should form part of the work done by children from primary school on.

(iii) It is not necessary to hold readings before a whole class. There can be times when the class is divided into groups, each member of each group giving his reading in turn. For preparation the groups have a different composition so that when the readings are finally performed no one has been present at anyone else's rehearsals, and so everyone is hearing the readings for the first time. Alternatively, of course, one class can prepare a programme for performance before another class, or before the whole school at, say, morning assembly or before a class in a neighbouring school. This kind of hierarchy of occasions varies the creative tension and keeps the activity fresh and stimulating: there is always an incentive, something to be worked towards, which gives point to what otherwise might become dull routine.

References and further reading

1. Katharine M. Briggs, *A Dictionary of British Folk-Tales in the English Language,* Routledge and Kegan Paul, 4 vols., 1970–71. A definitive work and a mine of sources useful to teachers. Expensive initial outlay, but cheap at the price; every school should have at least one set.
2. Alan Garner (ed.), *The Hamish Hamilton Book of Goblins,* Hamish Hamilton, 1969. Adaptations and retellings, a brilliantly edited collection drawn from folk lore of many lands. Garner's own reworking of 'Yallery Brown' (already mentioned and 'The Green Mist' haunt the memory and deserve frequent reading to children from mid-primary age onward.
3. Elizabeth Cook, *The Ordinary and the Fabulous,* Cambridge University Press, 1969. Subtitled 'An introduction to myths, legends and fairy tales for teachers and story tellers' and written in 'an attempt to show that a grown-up understanding of life is incomplete without an understanding of myths, legends and fairy tales; that the process of growing up would be harder and drearier without them; that there is an abundance of fabulous stories that are enjoyed by children of different ages, and that

there are innumerable ways of presenting them so that they become part and parcel of children's lives' (p. vii). Inspirational, informative, absorbingly readable: the kind of book for the teaching of teachers that has permanent value. The annotated book lists are exceptionally useful too.

4. Anthony Jones and June Buttrey, *Children and Stories*, Basil Blackwell, 1970. Theory and practice with the emphasis on practice. Written by working teachers, the text includes frequent examples drawn from classroom experience. Particularly useful for infant and primary school teachers.

5. Wallace Hildick, *Children and Fiction*, Evans, 1970. A critical study of 'the artistic and psychological factors involved in writing fiction for and about children', there are frequent digressions into the art of teaching fiction to children. Hildick was a teacher before he turned prolific writer for adults and children; he holds strong views and expresses them equally strongly. Always worth reading, even when one disagrees.

6. E. W. Hildick, Storypacks series, Evans, 1971. The four titles so far are: *Cokerheaton* (about a large town), *Rushbrook* (a village), *Musselton Bay* (a seaside town), *Gardeners Green* (a large new town). The packs include information, ideas, documents, pictures, and all kinds of 'realia' of the sort which an author needs in preparation for his creative work. The packs are intended as an open-ended starting point for children's oral and written work. The *Teacher's Book* provides a pedagogic guide.

7. Ruth Sawyer, *The Way of the Storyteller*, Viking Press, New York, Rev. ed. 1962. The Bodley Head, 1966. A classic on the subject, it 'transcends method and technique' but includes useful advice, especially on selection, and a chapter on 'Storytelling as an Approach to Children's Books and Reading'.

8. Mary Junor (ed.), *Stories to Tell*, Youth Libraries Group of the Library Association, London and Home Counties Branch, 1968. A short list in two sections (Picture Books and 'Stories') with annotations indicating how best to tell each tale. A basic collection of 27 volumes of sources for storytellers is included.

9. Janet Hill, *Children are People: The Librarian in the Community*, Hamish Hamilton, 1973. The children's librarian of the London Borough of Lambeth gives a detailed description of the storytelling activities in the borough, along with her personal views on the story-teller's art.

FIVE

Adult recommendations

There is a trap that people professionally responsible for the literary education of children fall into: the belief that there are certain books which children, whether they like and enjoy them or not, must be made to plod through in a kind of literary pilgrimage. Such cultural asceticism replaces 'ought' for 'like': the young 'ought' to read Dickens or Shakespeare or Eliot, William Mayne, Philippa Pearce or Lucy Boston. But if they are made to do so without liking what they read, then how far have we (and they) gone? How much nearer have we taken those young people towards the goal of true literacy? Not far, I think, and we may even have helped them to take a step or two away from it. The pleasure principle is the one that should guide the recommendations we make to children: we should make selections based on a clear understanding in our own minds of the facets of a book which we believe will be enjoyed by the children to whom we will offer it. This does not mean we shall always be in the position of suggesting books which have only minimal and crude attractions that pander to the baser side of the young. There are many different pleasures, as I've said before, to be had from literature. What we must be clear about on each occasion is which pleasures we will encourage a particular group of children to discover in the book we are recommending. To do this successfully demands certain things of us as teachers.

It requires first of all and above all that we balance intelligently two areas of knowledge in which we must become expert: intimate knowledge of the books available, children's and adult's, and intimate knowledge of the children to whom we are introducing the books we select. Knowledge of the books can only come from a conscientious reading of them for ourselves. This can be extensive but never complete; the difficulty is eased, however, by judicious use of reviews, book lists and authoritative surveys, the sources for which are included in the relevant section of this book.

Knowing the books is not of itself enough; those we decide to offer children must find a response in them. And this means we must acquire an ability to read as though we were the children we teach so that we read on one level as they do, discovering what they will enjoy, while on another level we assess how far a book will deepen literary awareness. A hard task. But one tempered by experience. Any critic has similar problems. He must read, so to speak, beyond his prejudices and personal tastes and be able to acknowledge the qualities in a piece of writing regardless of those biases. I have myself a well-known dislike for historical fiction; it is a genre that on the whole gives me little pleasure. But I hope this does not prevent my recognizing the fine things in Rosemary Sutcliff's work, for example, or Henry Treece's. And I would regard any attempt to sway children to my dislike as a form of cultural bullying as offensive in its own way as physical violence, not to say a betrayal of my responsibility as a teacher. Indeed, it is a professional duty to equip oneself sufficiently to be able to help a child along as a reader no matter what genre appeals to him, leading him from author to author, book to book, with enough sure-footed confidence so that he is guided up the literary mountain and not left wandering in the viewless foothills because of one's own incompetence.

Apart from these, other considerations should be remembered. We must learn to judge the occasion before recommending a book to children: its possibilities, 'mood', atmosphere. We must be ready to be flexible in our work, seizing the moment when it is ripe for introducing a book, and altering our methods to suit. Classes of children can sometimes prove to be stubbornly set against having anything to do with book introductions, and it is better then to engage them in other activities rather than be magistrally determined to have one's way and to go on in the face of their antagonism. At another time, the same classes may suddenly, for no apparent reason, be only too ready for such an occupation and then one needs (and here one's depth of knowledge comes in again) to be able to decide immediately which books to mention and how best in the circumstances to recommend them.

Whatever the situation, prepared for or unexpected, it is always too easy to over-play one's hand, praising a book so extravagantly, so effusively, that many children are put off. Uncritical gush is as repulsive as dry compulsion. A moderating honesty does no one any harm; all books have their flaws and it is just as wise to point these out as it is to draw attention to strengths and attractions, for children appreciate such integrity; when they find that their expectations have been time and again falsely raised they will react against teachers who mislead them. This is why it is best to let a book speak for itself as much as possible: a few comments followed by a brief but representative passage read aloud is better than a lot of talk about the book and how much one liked it, for then each child has a chance to size up the book for himself, letting his own antennae tell him whether it is something for him or not. Of course, there are times when everyone, children and adults, come across books that deeply please them, and then it is possible and right to express that great satisfaction; in this case the recommendation is credible because it is seen against a background of perhaps enthusiastic but certainly not indiscriminate praise.

Methods

BY-THE-WAY CONVERSATION

As much can be done outside the classroom as inside in recommending books to children. In break times, or a few minutes before or after school, during outings and 'educational visits', and in all the other social out-of-class situations, there are opportunities for suggesting books. And these occasions have the advantage of being relaxed, less formal, and particularly of being individual exchanges: teacher to child instead of teacher to group, so that the approach and the choice of books can fit the needs, capabilities, tastes, background and history of the children involved. No mystique surrounds this means of bringing children and books together; indeed, parents do precisely the same thing with their children, and people with each other, no matter what their ages. Though in the teacher's case it does mean that he is more watchful for opportunities and more aware of the reasons for his choice of recommendations. But the relationship should be just as natural. For I must strongly emphasize that I am not suggesting that teachers should be bibliographic bores, literary missionaries who blurt out titles and press books on children at every possible moment. One must choose the times and the frequency just as astutely as one must choose the books to suggest.

Following up such conversations is important. When a child shows a genuine interest in a book mentioned to him, a copy should be put into his hands as soon afterwards as possible. Avid young readers will more often than not search out a copy for themselves; but the less avid, and especially those who find reading difficult, need the kind of encouragement a teacher can give by taking enough care not just to mention books but to obtain copies for them. Nor should the matter rest there. After a while – enough time for the book to have been read – the child should be given a chance to talk about it; but again without this being pressed upon him if he prefers to say nothing. Equally, he should be allowed to dismiss a book summarily if that is all he feels it is worth. No one ought to be given the idea that these out-of-class encounters are simply curricula extension courses. When there is a give-and-take of opinion in which responses are honestly stated without imposition from the teacher, a continuous dialogue grows up between teacher and child as it does between two people sharing mutual interests, and so books are brought into the centre of everyday life, which, as I have stressed, is a basic condition in the education of young readers.

DISPLAYS AND EXHIBITIONS

Putting books on show is a way of making recommendations by, as it were, remote control. In the chapter on 'Set and Setting' I mentioned the way displays can help in creating a book-focal backdrop to daily life. But they do more than that. One teacher can work closely with only a few children; in a large school he may never even pass the time of day with the majority. Furthermore, it is an unpleasant but undeniable fact that some children will always find a teacher unattractive for all sorts of reasons, rational and irrational. Displays are a device by which he can reach out to both sections of the school community: children he doesn't know and those who don't much want to know him. When well organized and presented, displays take comparatively little time and effort compared with the value of their effect.

Like every method of recommendation, displays depend on two main ingredients: selection from the vast number of possible titles; and attractive lay-out, so that people will take notice of the books and want to know more about them. The primary rule to keep in mind is that displays work through visual appeal: the books selected, the decorative backgrounds, the legends, titles, and printed words – all must make an immediate impact on the eye. So colour, design, texture, shape need attention. It is no use throwing a few books together on a stand and hoping; some thought, care and skill are essential. There are other things to be kept in mind too:

1. Choice of site. A display set up in a dark corner of a busy corridor will receive little notice until it is knocked over. Plenty of light, with a display spot-light if possible, should illuminate the exhibition (a number of inexpensive, safe little spotlights intended for the job are now on the market). There should be plenty of room for people to stand and look without obstructing passers-by. And it is of benefit to place the display in such a position that whatever surrounds it draws the eye to it, rather than distracts. Displays should be centre-pieces: a matter of choice of site, and then of positioning within the site.

2. We can learn from good shopwindow displays and from the best museums about such matters as grouping of books shown, the number included (clutter is ugly; and overcrowding confuses the eye), the kind of materials to use for backgrounds, the use of space, different levels, and the massing of different shapes. Avoid anything tatty, botched-up and sloppily make-shift.

3. Initial impact is a key factor. This has two implications. First, every display should include some feature which has an eye-catching effect, and other features which hold the eye once it is caught. There are, in other words, two dimensions in any good show. Secondly, every display has a limited life-span. Once it has become too familiar, people cease to notice it is there at all and its usefulness is finished. It should be dismantled just before that moment is reached. The life-span varies according to the number of possible viewers, the site, and the complexity of the display. In a stable community like a school, judging when a display has reached its end is fairly easy; one simply keeps an eye on the number of times it is looked at and how much interest it generates. Once numbers and interest begin to flag then it is time to make a change.

4. Open displays (as opposed to those cased in or out of touching range) need daily maintenance. Things get moved and displaced, books tend to be taken away by those who cannot wait to read them, decorations get marked and damaged. Soon what began as an immaculate, well-presented show looks pretty tired.

5. Books on show ought to be available in copies for borrowing or buying, if possible. It is pointless to create interest if it is then allowed to dissipate because the books cannot be obtained; there is a correlation between length of time spent obtaining the book required and loss of interest.

6. A bit of peg-board with a few books hung precariously from wire hangers and the whole thing stuck on a wall is not good enough for a permanent display arrangement. Money is always short in schools, and exhibition stands are expensive. But commercial stands are not necessary. Very attractive settings can be put together out of all kinds of likely and unlikely objects. I have used the following as structures on which to mount displays: units from a Jacob's ladder (by permission of the caretaker!) built into an interesting shape, covered with sacking and decorated appropriately; packing cases used like building blocks and covered and painted as desired; gym gear, grouped, and decorated with netting from the cricket nets (it was winter and the nets were in store); art-room drawing tables and sketch boards; metal- and woodwork-shop benches and materials; tailor's dummies and stage platforms. Necessity mothers invention, and certainly invention in the presentation of books mothers surprised interest. And there are few departments within a school which do not possess or cannot produce objects that can be used as basic stands or as decorations to set off books.

7. Similarly, every department in a school qualifies as a useful site for an exhibition. Naturally, one thinks of sports novels in the gym and biographies of scientists in the labs. But that is a super-

ficial beginning; there is every reason for putting poetry in the gym and fantasy stories in the labs. But it is as well to remember whatever one does that for any kind of display outside one's own domain the willing cooperation of the relevant members of staff is an essential first step.

8. There are many variations on themes for displays. Some of the more common are:

(i) Collections of new books put out to inform people of their arrival and to create interest while new.

(ii) Books with a common denominator, such as novels about the sea, books about treasure-seeking, mystery stories, books by a single author, historical fiction about a particular event, period, etc., fiction and non-fiction about the same person, settings, etc.

(iii) In celebration of an occasion or an exploit topically in the news.

(iv) Books produced by one publisher, or in a series, or illustrated by the same artist.

(v) Award-winning books (the Carnegie medallists, *Guardian* and *T.E.S.* Information Book winners).

(vi) Books of the film, TV and radio adaptations, etc. – usually put on when the dramatization is showing locally.

(vii) Books reviewed in school magazine, library notes, class wall-newspapers, or chosen by panels of children.

Apart from book exhibitions there is supplementary value in displays of book-related material: the 'How a Book is Made' display from Brockhampton Press; photographs and potted biographies of authors (the Puffin Passports are excellent of this kind); originals and/or reproductions of illustrations and book jackets; work by children inspired by their reading (drawings, stories, poems, models, reports of visits to book settings).

All these are internally organized projects. Larger exhibits brought in from outside, from public library schools departments, the National Book League travelling collections, publishers' and booksellers' displays, require careful management and a special attempt to make them worth all the extra effort and often extra cost too by ensuring as good an audience as possible. This is why many teachers link them with special occasions such as PTA meetings and open days. Antony Kamm and Boswell Taylor describe very usefully this aspect of display organizing in their handbook *Books and the Teacher.* (1)

The quality and kind of displays – or the absence of them – in a school is a very accurate indicator of the value and place books hold in it. Certainly, if setting matters as much as I have suggested, and if teachers seek to recommend by more than in-class methods, displays will be a constant feature in the scenario.

IN-CLASS METHODS

I should say, first of all, that displays, of course, have a place in classrooms as well as in the open areas of a school. Teachers, regardless of a specialism (if they have one), should see that part of the setting they create in their own teaching areas is given up to books. This is one of the indirect methods by which they make recommendations.

Another indirect method is through class libraries and book boxes. No classroom should be without a fairly wide-ranging stock of books for reading by children at set times and in those moments when they are between jobs: when they have finished a piece of work and are waiting for attention, or as an interlude before starting something new, as well as for borrowing to take home. These stocks should consist of reference works of the standard kind – dictionaries, handbooks, concise encyclopaedias like the *Junior Pears*, some information books on topics in hand at the time – and of a selection of literature. This last is best put together from selections made by the teacher and added to by the children so that there is a feeling of corporate responsibility and interest in it. Through it, of course, by the titles each decides to put in, the teacher is actually recommending books to his children, as the children are to each other.

This class collection can be reinforced by what are in effect different forms of book lists and these are intended to lead children to books they can get from the central school library or from the public library. For example:

(i) 5″ × 3″ catalogue cards are kept in a 'Try These' file-drawer for pupils to consult when deciding on a book to read. Each card has written or typed on it a title, author, and brief annotation outlining plot, characters, and an indication of the kind of book – a blurb written by the teacher, or perhaps by a child who has read the book and suggested it. The cards can be arranged by subjects or by author or by any system that seems best in the situation.

(ii) 'Have you read these?' charts. These are large sheets of card or strong paper, containing book titles and short 'blurbs', presented attractively. The number of titles on each sheet need not be great; a number of sheets can be prepared and used in turn from a set which is carefully stored. The books selected can be organized just like displays by theme or subject, author or series, etc. And the sheets can be decorated with drawings, book jackets, children's comments about the titles included, photographs, etc.

(iii) Wall newspapers, class magazines and the like, produced by the children, can include a teacher's contribution in the form of a kind of review column in which he writes about books his 'readers'

might enjoy. (The same method is useful in the wider context of the
school magazine.)

Direct methods during class teaching time are most useful for
focusing attention on particularly important books which a teacher
especially wishes to encourage his children to read. These methods
are simple in outline, but they demand sensitive handling in
practice, as I've already indicated early in this chapter. The right
set must be stimulated, and the relationship between teacher and
taught must be receptive.

The most usual approach is for the teacher to show the chosen
book to his class. He spends a minute or two outlining what it is
about, though without giving away any details which would be
best enjoyed when met for the first time in a full reading, such as
twists in the plot, if it is a story, unexpected endings, and the like.
The aim is to whet the appetite, not to satisfy it. He may read an
extract aloud, show illustrations, and, in order to provide points of
comparison, refer to other books of a similar kind which he knows
some or all of his pupils have read. This may set off some children
who want to talk about the extract or about their reading as a
whole. Such an inclination ought to be encouraged because it leads
to the kind of discussion that makes reading a socially shared
experience as well as preparing the way for more formal literature
work. Once they have grown used to the method, children themselves can hold 'review' sessions in small groups or as a class,
telling each other about books they would like everyone to
read, an approach further discussed in chapter six, 'Friends and
peers'.

Many teachers make this kind of lesson a regular part of their
programme with all classes. Others are less regular, preferring to
do so only when they feel it is especially appropriate. I would not
myself want a set time on the time-table, but I do think it of sufficient importance and value to make sure an occasion is found every
few days for a session of 'book swopping' discussion.

In another style of lesson, the book is approached through film
clips, dramatizations on TV schools programmes, or played on
records or tapes made either commercially or by children who have
prepared and performed a 'radio' script version as an in- or out-of-
class project. Afterwards, these incidents, scenes, whole stories,
poems or plays are discussed, the original source always to hand and
available for children to borrow. Mechanically produced performances of this kind have peculiar advantages. To start with,
commercial films and recordings are made by people with professional resources not available to most teachers. Secondly, children
seem to attend with a different kind of intensity to electronic
pictures and sounds. Thirdly, the burden of stimulation is

removed from the teacher's shoulders, giving him a welcome respite. Everyone's personality and skills are limited and soon become familiar to people in contact with them every day; if no relief is given from them, this familiarity brings diminishing returns of interest unless the teacher is of unusual quality.

But there are basic details that need watching in the use of audio-visual aids, details which may seem commonsensical but which are also too often neglected. School classrooms are sometimes extraordinarily badly designed with poor acoustics, ineffective blackout facilities, and notoriously eccentric electrical outlets. Lessons that depend on a sensitive response to images – to literary language and imaginatively charged pictures – are ruined when inefficient equipment goes wrong or works with only crude results: hissing amplifiers, hazy film and TV screens, and the like. It is therefore a point of wisdom to ensure beforehand, no matter what the assurances given by technicians who are responsible for maintenance, that everything is in the best possible working order. Volume levels should be set at the beginning of the proceedings when the children are present because acoustics change with temperature and the number of people in a room as well as with the placing of loudspeakers. Then again, children like to be able to see the source of noise if there is no accompanying picture, so that tape or record-player speakers should be visible from all parts of the room. Naturally, having everyone in a position to see a screen in comfort must also be ensured.

A note on the sources of audio-visual material is appended to this chapter.

Introductory lessons of this sort may lead in secondary schools to close reading of books the children particularly enjoy: the directed study led by the teacher which lies outside the scope of this book. Indeed, some teachers use these methods to test out books which they would like to use as directed study texts, judging from the class's response the reception a book is likely to get in the more formal and lengthy curricula situation. In this way the lines between one approach and another blur, as they should, into a continuous, smooth programme of enjoyable work.

Records of reading

The general trends in reading activity in a school and certainly in a class are fairly easy to monitor: there are clear signs that give away what is happening, like the amount and quality of conversation between staff and pupils and among the pupils themselves about books, the keenness shown for new books, the rate of exchange in the central and class libraries. Less easy to monitor with comprehensive accuracy is the progress of individual children.

Every teacher has a fairly sure idea of the reading done by some pupils – the very keen and the very poor – and can guess at the diet of those in the middle ground. But this is putative, intuitive, reliant on dribs and drabs of information gleaned from conversation and observation. And it is not good enough to isolate in any reliable fashion the modulations of any one child's reading behaviour. To achieve this we need some kind of records.

No record system of a design which is practicable in relation to everything else a teacher must do in his working day will reveal all it would be useful to know; there are – thank goodness – areas of children's lives still private to themselves. School is by no means the only place where they acquire reading material. The best that records can do is to trace the effectiveness of the teacher's and the school's direct influence. Even so, this is not something to be dismissed lightly. Teachers who keep reading records find that the light the records throw on their work compensates for the irksomeness of the administrative chore of keeping them up to date.

When borrowed books must be charged in and out – as in libraries – no matter how rudimentary the system, maintaining records is relatively easy, a matter simply of routine clerical work. Some teachers have complained, when I make this point, that the work involved is nevertheless too taxing on their time. And so it will be if they try and do everything themselves. But keeping the kind of records I have in mind is something senior pupils in primary and secondary schools are quite capable of doing, and laying responsibility for the task on them makes sound educational as well as administrative sense. For several years I kept records of every child's daily borrowing in a five hundred plus secondary school; I cannot say that, with pupil help, I found this part of my job much of a strain, and the system could quite easily have coped with a far larger number of children.

These records were kept in squared column teacher's mark books. One double page lasted one class for a year. Down the side, the children's names were listed; across the top a column was allotted to each week of the school year, indicated by the week-ending date. Each main subject section of the library was given a letter symbol: 'Y' was the fiction section, 'D' the history section, etc. This made for simplification of the entries. Each time a book was borrowed the relevant symbol was entered in the record against the borrower's name and in the appropriate date column. This chore was done at the end of the day by the pupil-librarian on duty, who used the charging cards handed in by the borrower to get the necessary information. Thus, part of one page appears in the records like this:

Form: 2C																
1962-63	←Sept→			←Oct→					←Nov→					←Dec→		
Wkd	14	21	28	5	12	19	26		2	9	16	23	30	7	14	16
Blanch, Susan				Y	Y	Y	Y	Half term	Y		Y	Y		Y		
Davis, Howard				Y	Y	C			Y	Y	S			Y		
Day, Jennifer				Y	Y	Y			Y	Y		Y				
Hathaway, Stephen						Y										
Hollywell, Susan				Y	Y	Y	YY		Y	Y	Y	Y			YS	
Lugg, Terry				M		Y			M				Y		M	

FIG. 1

Certain information is at once clear to anyone, even those who
do not know the local conditions at that time. There are, for
instance, three school weeks gone before anyone borrows anything.
But once activity begins, Susan Blanch is a fairly steady customer,
taking only fiction books, the section favoured by most of the pupils
(only a selection of children are shown in Fig. 1, of course). Terry
Lugg, on the other hand, is a much less active borrower, though
more active than Stephen Hathaway, and takes books from the
science collection, the pure sciences at that (M). Susan Hollywell,
the most frequent borrower of all, on two occasions (26 October,
and 14 December) takes two books a week, one time taking,
unusually, something from the fine arts section. It is noticeable too
that these double borrowings occur just before holidays (half term
and the end of term) which suggests she plans her reading.

Two years later when these twelve plus year-olds were fourteen
plus and on the verge of leaving school – they were in a low stream
of a four stream secondary modern – their records looked like this:

Form: 4C																
1964-65	←Sept→			←Oct→					←Nov→				←Dec→			
Wkd	11	18	25	2	9	16	23	30	6	13	20	27	4	11		
Blanch, Susan	Y	F		F	F	YY	Y	Y	JY		JJ		Y	J		
Davis, Howard	X	S	D				X			Y	JS	F				
Day, Jennifer	F	S	F	YDF	XD	FX	JX		D		FF	F	F			
Hathaway, Stephen	YY		Y	YS							Y					
Hollywell, Susan		YRY	X	RY	RYY	FR	RR YJ	YRY	FR RYR	RRJ	FRJ	YYJ	RF JF	YJ		
Lugg, Terry	M	R		Y					M	S		Y	Y	Y		

FIG. 2

*N.B. Half term fell in part of a week, so that it does not show in the
records, as there was borrowing activity in the same week.*

Here again we get some interesting insights into these children
which would not have been so clear without the records. Overall,
the borrowing activity has increased considerably over the two
years; and this time it begins immediately term opens. Susan

Blanch has grown into a steady, totally fiction borrower who still finds a lot of books in the stock supplied by the school ('Y') but has begun to draw also from children's books ('J') and adult books ('F') supplied by the county library service. Jennifer Day selects almost completely from adult collections and has taken also some history and 'Fine Arts' books. Susan Hollywell, of course, shows up as the outstanding person. (I remember her well, a plump, comfortable and invariably cheerful girl, and the kind of voracious reader you don't need records to tell you about – though they are useful as a graph of her choices.) She is still very much a children's book borrower, though there are some adult books in her selection ('X', and 'F') with a smattering of titles taken from the applied sciences, which in Susan's case meant books on cookery and needlework. Stephen Hathaway is the problem child. He began his last year well enough, but as the year wore on and leaving day loomed up he became less interested than usual in anything to do with school. Stephen was a boy who found reading difficult, and no one ever quite managed to get him further than simple literacy.

There is in both sets of records a strong contrast between boys and girls, the girls being the regular and frequent borrowers taking mostly fiction and the boys being erratic and borrowing more non-fiction.

Overall these records were intended to reveal, and did, a number of factors:

1. The borrowing pattern for each child.
2. The borrowing pattern for the whole school.
3. The progress of the whole school and of individual children as the years passed.
4. The use made of the various main sections in the library.
5. The trends of boys' and girls' borrowing habits and preferences, and the contrast between them.
6. The classes where borrowing activity seemed below average, as a guide to where encouragement was especially needed.

Apart from such uses, however, records of this kind are valuable in suggesting approaches to individual children most in need of help. Stephen Hathaway is a perfect example.

Other kinds of records often employed are:

(i) Reading diaries kept by children themselves. They write down title and author and perhaps a short comment against the date when a book was finished.
(ii) A list of titles and authors of books borrowed from class libraries, book boxes, etc., which the teacher keeps, allotting one page of a notebook to each child.
(iii) A list of books in the class collection, kept in a squared mark book; the children tick off the square under their name and in line with the relevant title when they have read a book.

These devices all have their own advantages and disadvantages. When children are aware that records are kept there are always some who will want to impress or please and who therefore submit false reports, or borrow often without actually reading what they borrow. Indeed, all records are subject to this weakness: they record what was taken, not necessarily what was read by a child. And care must be taken to see that these teaching aids do not become weapons to brow-beat with: 'I see, Johnny, that you haven't borrowed a book for weeks – look at all these dreadful, empty squares! Now Sylvia has lots of entries under her name.' This sort of competitive blackmail does nothing but exacerbate the problems that hinder poor readers and feed the base egos of those held up for praise – who are thereby also taught the benefits of sycophancy. Records are not a literary means test and are best kept by the teacher for his own professional use only.

Furthermore, no record of borrowing or of 'personal reading' based on books supplied by the school is ever a full account of all a child has actually read. Books from public libraries, bought from shops, borrowed from friends, given as presents; magazines, newspapers, comics: none of these find a place. From time to time it is worth a teacher's while to acquaint himself with a fuller picture of his pupils' reading habits by asking them to answer the following questions on a slip of paper:

(a) *List the newspapers you have looked at and read during the last week.* ('Read' needs careful definition each time!)

(b) *Do you read them regularly?*

(c) *List the magazines and comics you have read during the last week. Do you read them regularly?*

(d) *Write down the titles of all the books you have read in the last fortnight* (a week is rarely a good time-unit for book reading profiles) *no matter where you got the books from.*

(e) *Write down anything else you remember reading over the last week which you haven't so far mentioned.*

Such a questionnaire may not be strictly scientific and its results only of local use. But linked to the teacher's personal knowledge of the children involved, and all the circumstances surrounding his work, this kind of reflection of a class's present reading patterns is of great help in making connections between their spontaneous interests and knowledge and the approaches made in teaching them.

A final note to end this chapter. No teacher needs to, or ought to, work alone in recommending books to children. There are others who can be brought in, either to advise the teacher himself – even if that means only an exchange of views and a swopping of notes about books and methods – or to work with the children. One

begins at home, of course, getting other members of staff to promote books. But there are outsiders who can be brought in as
guests: authors, illustrators, public librarians, booksellers, publishers, L.E.A. advisers, H.M.I.s, and parents – anyone who by
their presence and refreshing unfamiliarity can change the pace of
the everyday encounters between teacher and taught, and can show
by what they are and say that books and reading have a vital and
important place in their lives. I have called these guests 'Star
Performers' and have examined their contribution and the way
teachers can organize visits in chapter nine.

Sources of audio-visual material

Despite the emphasis put these days on the value of audio-visual
materials – perhaps, indeed, because of the rapid growth in these
resources – there are few guides of a comprehensive and critically
detailed character available to teachers. It is a task being tackled
in various quarters, but until there are published results we must
find our way as best we can among the proliferating manufacturers,
publishers and suppliers. I hope the following information is at
least of some help in indicating where one might begin.

1. Always first check the audio-visual stocks held in one's own
   school and education and library authorities. More and more
   L.E.A.s are building up central stocks which their schools may
   borrow free of charge; libraries have growing collections of
   material; and individual schools vary in the organization of
   their audio-visual resources. Knowledge of what is available
   locally can save hours of lost time searching the country through
   the post, as well as money spent hiring from commercial loan
   firms.
2. The Educational Foundation for Visual Aids (EFVA) and the
   National Committee for Audio-Visual Aids in Education,
   33 Queen Anne Street, London, W1M OAL (01–636 5742 and
   5791) publish catalogues of the most comprehensive range and
   these can be bought, either to aid teachers in their own resource
   buying or ,from which to select material that can be borrowed
   from the National Audio-Visual Aids Library, Paxton Place,
   Gypsy Road, London SE27 9SR (01–670 4247/9).
   The most useful catalogues relating to this book are:
   Audio Visual Aids (Film strips, films, transparencies, wallsheets
       and recorded sound) *Part 1*: Religious Education, English,
       Modern Languages.
   Records and Tapes for Education.
   Wallcharts.
   8mm Cassette Loop Films.

3. *Film*

The most immediately useful hire libraries loaning out 16mm film are the following:

Children's Film Foundation. Distributed by Rank Film Library (see below).

Columbia Pictures (16mm division), 142 Wardour Street, London W1. (Catalogue 50p).

Connoisseur Films, 167 Oxford Street, London W1. (Catalogue 25p).

Rank Film Library, P.O. Box 70, Great West Road, Brentford, Mddx. (Catalogue 25p).

Film clips (short extracts from long films, usually of one scene, incident, or sequence, and useful for close study or as a dramatized introduction to a book): these may be obtained from some of the above libraries as well as from: The National Film Archive, 81 Dean Street, London W1V 6AA.

Film strips. The following firm specializes in strips and films made from children's books:

Weston Woods Studios Ltd., P.O. Box 2, Henley on Thames, Oxford.

4. *Recordings*

A considerable number and variety of spoken-word recordings on disc and tape are available. A complete and regularly revised catalogue can be obtained from:

The Gramophone (Spoken word and miscellaneous catalogue, 35p), 177–179 Kenton Road, Kenton, Harrow, Mddx. HA3 OHA.

5. *Wallcharts*

In support of the EFVA catalogue obtain:

Posters and Paraphernalia, included in *Children's Book Review* Vol II, No. 4, Sept. 1972, from Five Owls Press, 67 High Road, Wormley, Broxbourne, Herts.

6. Complete list of known distributors working in this field (not all these, of course, will provide book-related material, though those starred [*] are known to be of help in this regard):

*ABBEY RECORDING CO. LTD, Abbey Street, Eynsham, Oxford.

*ANGLO EMI FILM DISTRIBUTORS LTD, Film House, 142 Wardour Street, London, W1V 4AE.

*ARGO RECORD CO. LTD, 113–115 Fulham Road, London, SW3.

ATTICO FILMS, 27 Church Street, Wath-upon-Dearne, Rotherham, Yorks.

*BBC PUBLICATIONS, London, W1A 1AR.

BBC RADIO ENTERPRISES (REB, REC, REGL and REM series records), Villiers House, Haven Green, London, W5.

BBC RADIO ENTERPRISES (RESR series records), London, SE99.

BBC TV ENTERPRISES, Educational and Training Film Sales, Villiers House, Haven Green, London, W5.

*BBC TV ENTERPRISES FILM HIRE, 25 The Burroughs, Hendon, London, NW4.

BLACKIE AND SON LTD, Bishopbriggs, Glasgow.

BODLEIAN LIBRARY, Assistant Librarian, Department of Western MSS, Oxford.

BOULTON-HAWKER FILMS LTD, Hadleigh, Ipswich, Suffolk.

*BRITISH FILM INSTITUTE, 81 Dean Street, London, W1.

BRITISH TRANSPORT FILMS, Melbury House, Melbury Terrace, London, NW1.

BRODIE'S EDUCATIONAL FILMSTRIPS LTD, Brodie House, Queen Square, Bath, Somerset.

*BRUNSWICK DECCA RECORD CO. LTD, 9 Albert Embankment, London, SE1.

CAMERA TALKS LTD, 31 North Row, London, W1R 2EN.

CAPITOL, THE GRAMOPHONE CO. LTD, 20 Manchester Square, London, W1.

CARWAL AUDIO-VISUAL AIDS, P.O. Box, 55 Wallington, Surrey.

CATHOLIC FILM INSTITUTE: distributed by St Paul Publications, St Paul's House, Middle Green, Langley, Bucks.

CBS RECORDS, 28–30 Theobalds Road, London, WC1.

CENTAUR BOOKS LTD, 284 High Street, Slough, Bucks.

CFL, CENTRAL FILM LIBRARY, Government Building, Bromyard Avenue, Acton, London, W3.

CHESHIRE FOUNDATION HOMES, The Secretary, 7 Market Mews, London, W1Y 8HP.

CHRISTIAN AID/THE BRITISH COUNCIL OF CHURCHES, Films and Publications Dept, 2 Sloane Gardens, London, SW1.

CHRISTIAN BROADCASTING COMMISSION, Hawkley Studios, Nr Liss, Hants.

CHURCH OF SCOTLAND AVA DISTRIBUTION CENTRE, 121a George Street, Edinburgh, EH2 4YN.

CHURCH UNION, Church Literature Association, 199 Uxbridge Road, London, W12.

COLLET RECORDS, 39 Museum Street, London, WC1.

*COLUMBIA PICTURES CORPORATION, 142 Wardour Street, London, W1.

COMMON GROUND FILMSTRIPS, Longman Group, Pinnacles, Harlow, Essex.

*CONCORD FILMS COUNCIL, Nacton, Ipswich, Suffolk.

CONCORDIA FILMS, Concordia House, 117–123 Golden Lane, London, EC1Y OTL.

*CONTEMPORARY FILMS LTD, 55 Greek Street, London, W1V 6DB.

*DECCA RECORD CO. LTD, 9 Albert Embankment, London, SE1.

DELYSE, PYE RECORDS LTD, ATV House, 17 Great Cumberland Place, London, W1.

DISC IMPORTS LTD, 36 John Dalton Street, Manchester 2.

DISCOURSES LTD, 34 High Street, Royal Tunbridge Wells, Kent.

DISCURIO, WILLIAM LEONARDS CONCERTS LTD, 9 Shepherd Street, London, W1.

EALING SCIENTIFIC LTD, Greycaine Road, Watford, WD2 4PW.

*EAV, EDUCATIONAL AUDIO-VISUAL LTD, 38 Warren Street, London, W1.

EDUCATIONAL AND TELEVISION FILMS LTD, 2 Doughty Street, London, WC1.

EDUCATIONAL FILMS OF SCOTLAND, 16–17 Woodside Terrace, Charing Cross, Glasgow, C3.

EDUCATIONAL PRODUCTIONS LTD, East Ardsley, Wakefield. Yorks.

EDUCATIONAL SUPPLY ASSOCIATION, Pinnacles, Harlow, Essex.

*EFVA, THE NATIONAL AUDIO-VISUAL AIDS LIBRARY, Paxton Place, Gipsy Road, London, SE27 9SR.

EMBER RECORDS, Suite 4, Carlton Tower Place, Sloane Street, London, SW1.

EMI, 20 Manchester Square, London, W1.

ENCYCLOPAEDIA BRITANNICA INTERNATIONAL LTD, 18–20 Regent Street, London, SW1.

ENGLISH UNIVERSITIES PRESS LTD, 8 Warwick Lane, London, EC4.

EOTHEN FILMS (INTERNATIONAL) LTD, 70 Furzehill Road, Boreham Wood, Herts.

ERA: distributed by Discourses Ltd, 34 High Street, Royal Tunbridge Wells, Kent.

ERNEST BENN LTD, Bouverie House, Fleet Street, London, EC4A 2DL.

EUROPEAN SCHOOLBOOKS LTD, 100 Great Russell Street, London, WC1.

FACT AND FAITH FILMS, Falcon Court, 32 Fleet Street, London, EC4.

*FILM DISTRIBUTORS ASSOCIATED (16 mm) LTD, 37–41 Mortimer Street, London, W1A 2JL.

FOLKWAYS, TRANSATLANTIC RECORDS LTD, 86 Marylebone High Street, London, W1M 4AY.

FONTANA, PHILIPS RECORDS LTD, Stanhope House, Stanhope Place, London, W2.

FREDERICK WARNE AND CO. LTD, Educational Dept. Chandos House, Bedford Court, Bedford Street, Strand, London, WC2.

GATEWAY EDUCATIONAL FILMS LTD, St Lawrence House, 29–31 Broad Street, Bristol, BS1 2HF.

HARRAP AUDIO-VISUAL AIDS, P.O. Box 70, 182 High Holborn, London, WC1.

HERALD SACRED RECORDINGS, WORD UK LTD, Greycaine House, Greycaine Road, Watford, WD2 4PW.

*HMV, The GRAMOPHONE CO. LTD, 20 Manchester Square, London, W1.

HULTON EDUCATIONAL PUBLICATIONS LTD, Raans Road, Amersham, Bucks.

HUNTER FILMS LTD, 182 Wardour Street, London, W1V 4BH.

JOHN KING (FILMS) LTD, Film House, 71 East Street, Brighton, BN1 1NZ.

JNF, JEWISH NATIONAL FUND, Rex House, 4–12 Regent Street, London, SW1.

JOHN WRIGHT AND SONS LTD, The Stonebridge Press, Bath Road, Bristol, 4.

*JONATHAN CAPE LTD, 30 Bedford Square, London, WC1.

JUPITER RECORDINGS LTD, 140 Kensington Church Street, London, W8.

UNIVERSITY OF LEEDS: distributed by The National Audio-Visual Aids Library, Paxton Place, Gipsy Road, London, SE27 9SR.

LEOMARK: distributed by SPCK Audio-Visual Aids Dept, 69 Great Peter Street, London, SW1.

The LINGUAPHONE INSTITUTE, 207 Regent Street, London, W1.

LISTEN RECORDS: distributed by Discourses Ltd, 34 High Street, Royal Tunbridge Wells, Kent.

*LIVING SHAKESPEARE, ODHAMS BOOKS, Brasted, Sevenoaks, Kent.

LIVINGSTON RECORDINGS, WORD UK LTD, Greycaine House, Greycaine Road, Watford, WD2 4PW.

LONDON MISSIONARY SOCIETY, 11 Carteret Street, London, SW1.

*LONGMAN GROUP LTD, Pinnacles, Harlow, Essex.

MACDONALD AND EVANS LTD, 8 John Street, London, W1.

MACDONALD EDUCATIONAL, BPC PUBLISHING LTD, St Giles House, 49–50 Poland Street, London, W1A 2LG.

*MACMILLAN AND CO. LTD, Brunel Road, Basingstoke, Hants.

MARIAN RAY, 36 Villiers Avenue, Surbiton, Surrey.

METHODIST MISSIONARY SOCIETY, Home Organization Dept, 25 Marylebone Road, London, NW1.

MICRO METHODS LTD, East Ardsley, Wakefield, Yorks.

MILLER, MILLER'S MUSIC CENTRE LTD, Sidney Street, Cambridge.

*NATIONAL AUDIO-VISUAL AIDS LIBRARY, Paxton Place, Gipsy Road, London, SE27 9SR.

NATIONAL CHRISTIAN EDUCATION COUNCIL, Robert Denholm House, Nutfield, Redhill, Surrey.

NATIONAL COAL BOARD, Film Branch, 68–70 Wardour Street, London, W1.

NATIONAL FILM BOARD OF CANADA, 1 Grosvenor Square, London, W1.

T. NELSON AND SONS LTD, 36 Park Street, Park Lane, London, W1.

NUFFIELD FOUNDATION FOREIGN LANGUAGE TEACHING MATERIALS PROJECT, University of York, Micklegate House, Micklegate, York, YO1 1JZ.

OVERSEAS MISSIONARY FELLOWSHIP, Newington Green, London, N16.

PARLOPHONE, THE GRAMOPHONE CO. LTD, 20 Manchester Square, London, W1.

W. PAXTON AND CO. LTD, 36–38 Dean Street, London, W1.

PERGAMON PRESS LTD, Headington Hill Hall, Oxford, OX3 OBW.

PHILIP AND TACEY LTD, 69–79 Fulham High Street, London, SW6.

PHILIPS RECORDS LTD, Stanhope House, Stanhope Place, London, W2.

*PICTORIAL CHARTS EDUCATIONAL TRUST, 132–8 Uxbridge Road, London, W13.

PSYCHE, SAGA RECORDS LTD, 326 Kensal Road, London, W10.

PYE RECORDS (SALES) LTD, ATV House, 17 Great Cumberland Place, London, W1H 8AA.

*RANK AUDIO-VISUAL LTD, P.O. Box 70, Great West Road, Brentford, Middx.

RCA LTD, 50 Curzon Street, London, W1Y 8EU.

RELIGIOUS EDUCATION PRESS LTD, Headington Hill Hall, Oxford.

RELIGIOUS FILMS LTD, 6 Eaton Gate, London, SW1.

RON HARRIS CINEMA SERVICES LTD, Glenbuck House, Glenbuck Road, Surbiton, Surrey.

ROYAL NETHERLANDS EMBASSY: distributed by The National Audio-Visual Aids Library, Paxton Place, Gipsy Road, London, SE27 9SR.

SAGA RECORDS LTD, 326 Kensal Road, London, W10.

SCFL, SCOTTISH CENTRAL FILM LIBRARY, 16–17 Woodside Terrace, Charing Cross, Glasgow, C3.

SCOTTISH RECORDS, 52 Bon Accord Street, Aberdeen, Scotland.

SCRIPTURE UNION BOOKSHOP, AVA Loans, 5 Wigmore Street, London, W1H OAD.

SOUND SERVICES LTD, Kingston Road, Merton Park, London, SW19.

SPCK, Audio-Visual Aids Dept, 69 Great Peter Street, London, SW1.

*SPORTS FILMS, Eskdale, Totteridge Lane, London, N20.

*STUDENTS RECORDINGS LTD, King Street, Newton Abbot, Devon.

SUNDAY TIMES, Thomson House, 200 Gray's Inn Road, London, WC1.

SUSSEX TAPES, 62 Queens Grove, London, NW8 6ER.

TRANSAID, FRANCIS GREGORY AND SON LTD, Spur Road, Feltham, Middx.

TRANSATLANTIC RECORDS Ltd, 86 Marylebone High Street, London, W1M 4AY.

TUTOR-TAPE CO. LTD, 2 Replingham Road, London, SW18.

UNITED SOCIETY FOR CHRISTIAN LITERATURE, 4 Bouverie Street, London, EC4.

UNIVERSITY OF LONDON PRESS LTD, Saint Paul's House, Warwick Lane, London, EC4.

*VISUAL EDUCATION LTD, Hawkley Studios, Liss, Hants.

VISUAL INFORMATION SERVICE LTD, 12 Bridge Street, Hungerford, Berks.

VISUAL PUBLICATIONS, 197 Kensington High Street, London, W8.

*WESTON WOODS STUDIOS LTD, P.O. Box 2, Henley-on-Thames, Oxford.

WILLS AND HEPWORTH LTD, Loughborough, Leics.

Reference
1. Antony Kamm and Boswell Taylor, *Books and the Teacher*, University of London Press, 2nd ed. 1970. A useful handbook about the production of books and their use in schools; includes an extensive reference section where publishers' addresses, book lists and printing information can be found.

SIX

Friends and peers

No one needs to be told that children wield powerful persuasive influences upon each other; the fact that they do is not only observable every day, it is part of everyone's childhood experience. The friends children make, the peer groups they belong to – whether the Boy Scouts, the neighbourhood gang, or simply a loose association of acquaintances who do things together now and again – have one result that matters in the context of this book. By a kind of fission process, a chain reaction, the young pass on from one to another their enthusiasms and concerns, their attitudes, interests and modes of behaviour. How can we put some of this fission energy to work on behalf of children's reading? How can we channel it so that children help each other through the network of social relationships which so much affect their likes and dislikes, their disposition to engage in activities which are approved of and enjoyed by their contemporaries?

There are some techniques we can use that propel us in the right direction, provided that we have first of all created a set and setting (see chapter two) favourable for them to work in. On their own, none of these techniques gets very far. But as part of a much larger programme they add a dimension that cannot be achieved in any other way. For what we are trying to do through them is to make reading an activity promoted by children among themselves, in the same way that they promote among themselves interests in, for example, certain games, fashions of clothes and music.

'HAVE YOU READ THIS?' SESSIONS
These are lesson times when children share their opinions about books they have read, recommending them to others. They can be organized in different ways, but the two-fold effects are the same: the discussions make reading (which tends to be a private pleasure) into a social activity; and particular books are mentioned which others might be led to read for themselves. The sessions may come about *en passant* and spontaneously: Gail mentions to her teacher that she has just finished a book she very much enjoyed; she is asked there and then to tell the others about it. Or they may be set times, prepared for beforehand by teacher and pupils, each of whom decides on the books he wants to talk about and what he wants to say about them. Then in small groups or as a whole class

together the children take it in turn to make their recommendations, conducting afterwards a discussion to which anyone who wants can contribute comments. Copies of the books mentioned are shown around, and are borrowed by those who feel they would like to read them.

However the sessions come about, the teacher has a sensitive problem in judging how much to take part: when to stay out of the discussion and when to have his say, when to guide and challenge and when to let the conversation follow its own path unhindered. He will be particularly employed, of course, as a chairman, seeing that the floor is not hogged by a few articulate public speakers. And he can perhaps best contribute by feeding into the discussions references drawn from his wider reading experience and book-knowledge, helping to add depth and range to what is said and recommended. The unhappy tendency among teachers – an occupational neurosis – is to jump in too early and too often, especially if the talk wanders from direct comments about books under consideration, as though they have not realized that, except for carefully prepared debate, all talk now and then wanders down by-ways, for a moment or two, during which the participants gather themselves for a fresh attack on the main subject. It may sometimes be necessary for a teacher to bring a discussion back to the work in hand when it gets lost in a maze of trivia. But to prevent any meandering at all, or to dam the flow of talk too soon and too often by intruding, generally only frustrates the spontaneity wherein lies the pleasure and the educative value of this activity.

Certainly, at the end of these prepared sessions the teacher should consolidate what has been said in order to focus attention on the primary purpose of the technique: getting children to read books. ('John's group discussed *The Overland Launch* by C. Walter Hodges,' he may say, holding up a copy, 'a story based on fact about a life-boat that had to be dragged across rough country before it could be put into the sea to rescue a ship in distress. John said he thought the story much more exciting than he had expected it would be. Susan's group looked at *The Borrowers* by Mary Norton . . . during which Helen mentioned how much she enjoyed reading *Charlotte's Web* by E. B. White in which . . .' And so on.)

Variations can be built on this basic idea. A book-panel composed of members of one class can record a discussion on tape for playing to another class in the same age year: a kind of radio book review programme. Readings of extracts prepared by other children can help to exemplify what is said, and the choosing of relevant passages involves a class in considerable, but purposeful, literary criticism. A senior group may do the same sort of programme about books they remember with pleasure from the time when they were, say, eleven, and the tape can be played to children of that age. This sort of approach can be used between schools who share each other's tapes. Alternatively the programme can be given 'live' before an 'audience' who then add their own comments to the things said by the 'panel'. Again, this can go on between classes, between years in one school, and between schools of similar or different kinds.

Another method is to put children into small groups and leave them alone to talk about books they have read. Recent experiments held throughout the country have shown how responsive children are when handled like this. Recordings made of sessions reveal how little idle chatter goes on, and how excited in a controlled way the exchanges become. Success partly depends on a teacher's skill in putting together the right children, as well as on the care taken in preparing everyone for what is going to happen.

In my view, the mutual sharing of reading experiences through conversation of these kinds is the best method of all by which peer influences can be organized and channelled. As the child quoted by Andrew Stibbs in his article reprinted in Appendix Three says: 'When books are recommended by your own age group you tend to go for those rather than the ones a teacher would recommend.'

BOOK REVIEWS

As drill exercises in writing, or as a check that children have actually read what they say they have read, the writing of book reviews has little to commend it. Their only proper purpose is that they shall be read by others. Having made this prefatory warning, it has also to be said that many teachers successfully contrive to make reviewing an enjoyable and useful ingredient in their book and reading programme. The key to their success is publication. Reviews must be made available to their authors' peers. An obvious outlet is the wall newspaper, another is the school magazine. Some teachers keep a library or class journal going devoted to 'literary magazine' material (reviews, stories, poems, articles about books, etc.). And there is the Review Folder: a loose-leaf file into which specially good reviews are put for permanent keeping and use. Any child who wants help in choosing a book is allowed to read through the folder to see if it suggests anything to him.

Anyone who has written reviews professionally knows how difficult it is to do the job well. Even in the basic form of bibliographic details, outline of content, response to content, and evaluation and comparison against other books of similar kind, a review is a very formal and structured essay. To infuse into that basic form an element of linguistic liveliness and wit, which marks out the best adult reviewers, is to ask far more than most children can hope to achieve. And so it seems to me that reviews we ask children to write should not be rigid in form. In many cases they may be no more than a short comment. Certainly by the end of primary school or the beginning of secondary school children should understand what a good conventional review is like; but it is not necessary for them to be able to write one before their written comments on books can be used with their peers.

Again, there are variations. Some teachers put into the backs of books in their class libraries slips of paper on which children may write short comments. Those who think this practice defaces a book use instead a review catalogue: a drawer of five-by-three cards, each bearing the book's title and author, on which comments can be written. Or a large sheet of lined paper is put up on the wall, and children can write things on it under the appropriate title. These methods are particularly useful with younger children who are not yet able to write long passages.

MAGAZINES

These may be ephemeral, like wall newspapers, or more permanent, like the school magazine. They are less limited than review slips or files in that different approaches can be allowed: poems, short stories, potted biographies about authors, illustrations of scenes or characters, accounts of visits to places described in stories, like Alderley Edge in *The Weirdstone of Brisingamen* by Alan Garner or Arthur Ransome's Norfolk Broads in his *Coot Club*, or the Shropshire settings used a number of times by Malcolm Saville in his Lone Pine mysteries. In this kind of work, everything is book-based and may be tangential in recommending books to children, but frequently it is the effect a book has on someone else that leads us to read it, rather than anything said about the book itself.

An aid that should not be neglected at primary or secondary level is *Puffin Post*, the hotch-potch magazine put out by Puffin Books. The *Post* cannot be faulted as a children's book magazine: colourful, bubbling with energy and fun, full of jokes, cartoons, illustrations, games, competitions, stories, poems, children's book reviews, articles about writers, and, because of its coded messages and esoteric tone, touched with the flavour of a secret society. Of course it is also a vehicle for advertising Puffin Books, but with its first number seven years ago it transcended any mere commercial connivance and has now grown into a national institution that probably does a very great deal to encourage literate reading among the young. The feeling of lively enjoyment you get from the *Post*'s pages stands in sharp contrast to the brackish dullness that surrounds books in too many schools. It demonstrates what children can feel for reading, what can be achieved with them, and how to go about achieving it.

Individual membership of the Puffin Club brings the magazine four times a year, a badge and other essentials of such organizations, and costs 50p per year. Schools can enter a corporate subscription for 38p per pupil, provided twenty or more children join and that there is one person responsible for receiving and distributing the magazine. Write to: The Puffin Club Secretary, Penguin Books Ltd, Harmondsworth, Middlesex.

SELECTION PANELS

Every chance should be taken of involving children in choosing books intended for them to read: in class and school libraries, for sale in school bookshops, and for displays and exhibitions.

The act of reaching decisions requires discussion, sharing of opinions, suggestions, reading done. If the panel members represent class groups, they must canvass for suggestions; if an entire group is involved, debate can be formally organized and kept going informally out of class by the teacher asking individual children their opinions. This kind of activity especially promotes controversy: there is competition to get one's own title into the final list, and argument about this book being better than that. Children find themselves taking sides about what they have read or want to read: an entirely healthy situation worth a lot of conventional teaching time.

If they are allowed, however, these selection methods must genuinely be what they claim to be, and not simply a front behind which the teacher does as he likes regardless of what the children decide. He can, after all, draw the limits, retaining for himself the right to veto or to select a certain proportion of the stock on his own. But the limitations set must be clearly defined before the panels go to work. And certainly, before selection meetings, there should be ample time for the children to argue among themselves. It is useful if exhibitions can be mounted or visits made to the public library or bookshops where a range of titles can be seen and browsed through. Children need to make informed suggestions as much as adults in book selection.

When all these techniques have been accepted and enjoyed, some critical questions that demand discussion will arise. How do you judge a book? What are you looking for when selecting for other people? What language helps you to make your thoughts about books clear? Are some books better than others? In what ways? How do you know? What is it you get from reading a work of literature? Are there different ways of reading? What are they? When such questions crop up naturally children are well on the road towards becoming literate readers. And their teachers can begin to make them aware of what is happening. Ideally, this point will be reached by early secondary school level, which means that steady work of the kind I've been describing must be carried on through the primary school years.

So these apparently superficial and peripheral activities, practised in tandem with techniques outlined elsewhere in this book, lead directly to three centrally important elements in the making of literary readers: a vital social atmosphere that creates individual reading interests; the widening and deepening of children's own reading; and the articulation of responses – what in other contexts we would call criticism.

To these classroom methods, we can add two out-of-class features that lead in the same direction.

PUPIL ORGANIZERS

When people, no matter what their age, are involved in the organization of affairs, and especially when they have responsibility for at least part of the organization, their involvement, their commitment, tends to be greater, keener, than otherwise, and they tend to proselytize. In every school, from infants onwards, there are opportunities for children to help with the organization and provision of books: in class and central libraries, in specialist collections, in putting on displays and exhibitions, in ordering and preparing stocks, in running the bookshop, in promotion and publicity, and the like. One example will demonstrate the potential – the minimum potential – for this kind of involvement.

A secondary school of five hundred boys and girls with a central library stock of 6,000 volumes and a number of class and specialist libraries under its wing provided opportunities for the following pupil staff:

2 'senior librarians';

15 'school librarians';

40 'class librarians' – two a class;

6 'specialist librarians' looking after collections in the science department, craft department and main English room.

Their jobs divided up like this: of the fifteen school librarians, two seniors were in charge (one boy, one girl). Their duties as listed in the duplicated handbook issued to each pupil-librarian were:

1. To supervise the librarians.
2. To arrange duty rosters.
3. To make up the records daily (i.e. of books issued, etc.)
4. To come in before school each morning and check:
   (a) that the date stamp was set correctly
   (b) that the library was tidy and presentable.
5. To check on overdue books.

6. To see that work was prepared for the duty librarian to do during break and lunchtime.
7. To arrange for the decoration of the library: e.g. flowers, displays, etc.
8. To check daily with the teacher-librarian that all was in order and to receive instructions.
9. To arrange for and conduct library staff meetings weekly.
10. To train and examine pupil-librarians during their probationary period.
11. To liaise with and supervise class and specialist librarians.

This represents a considerable work load and requires a good deal of thought, time and energy from sixteen-year-olds. But that was intentional. Because so much was demanded, as much was given: the job was worth having. Naturally, there were lapses and mistakes, and senior librarians varied in quality. But all of them did their utmost and knew that their position was a key one within the school.

The ordinary 'school librarians' began their work in the second year and could remain on the staff until they left school. They took turns in supervising the library in and out of school hours. In pairs, they looked after the condition of one section of the stock or had other areas of responsibility under the seniors. Everything, in fact, including discipline within the library was looked after by these young people. The teacher-librarian's job was wholly supervisory, with the exception of actually buying new stock, classifying and accessing it.

The class and specialist librarians did with their smaller collections precisely what the school librarians did with the central collection, and attended the weekly staff meetings. They also knew the system in the central library so well that when their classes were in the main library there was always someone present who could answer routine administrative questions.

The educational potentials of such a system are obvious; its pertinence here is that it charges the social atmosphere of a school with a peer group and individuals whose concerns for books are practical, of daily importance. Their influence on the set and setting of the rest of the school is tentacular, reaching into every class, every curricular department. They are a cell, a ginger group, a leaven.

Clearly, younger children would be unable to cope with the whole range of responsibilities and jobs borne by these secondary-school-aged children; but there is still plenty that they can do even if under closer teacher supervision, with the same results. No matter how sophisticatedly professional and adult is the organization of school book stocks, or, at the other extreme, how young the children, it is, in my view, negligence of the worst kind to shut out pupils from an organization that is intended to benefit them and to help create in them a book consciousness. The emphasis should always be on the use of book stocks as an instrument to develop literary skills and the promotion of reading, rather than on bibliographic and library niceties that suit the British Museum and higher academic research more than they encourage a book-loving body of children. (See chapter eight on book ownership for the place of the school bookshop in this scheme.)

BOOK CLUBS

Some teachers argue against book clubs, claiming that they bring together only a certain kind of avid reader, the literary equivalent of the religiously effete and over-pious. It is a danger; but it ought also to be said that school clubs invariably reflect the style and manner of the teachers who run them. Book clubs do not have to be cliquish, pretentious, stuffily self-inflated, or bolt-holes for ethereal literary spirits. On the straightforward point that they bring together only avid readers, it seems to me of great importance that children who are keen readers should have a chance to meet together. We do not regard such a thing as at all odd when hobbyists meet; rather, we encourage it. Bookish children, as they tend somewhat negatively to be called, deserve at least as much nurturing.

That apart, book clubs need not be enclosed, much less ingrown: one of their aims ought to be to mount open meetings which will attract non-members. A club should be a hub at the centre of all the book-based activities involving the rest of the school. And the atmosphere, especially in primary schools, should be celebratory, the events more akin to a literary workshop than to a W.E.A. lecture course. Talks on this and that aspect of books are all very well, but they can be overdone. Things like the following should be included on the programme: play-making; writing, illustrating; magazine production; readings; story-tellings; film shows; visits to exhibitions, etc. (the Children's Book Show held yearly in different parts of the country, for example) parties (numerous hints in *Puffin Post*); book sales; book fairs; recording dramatizations; model-making on book-themes. Obviously a great deal depends on the age of the children and their circumstances. But the aim is to create another cell within the body of the school, in this case composed of hard-core readers who are sustained by the club meetings and who establish a social book-centre. Like the librarians and the bookshop staff, the club members are catalysts who spark off that fission from which will spread from child to child an awareness of books and the habit of reading them.

SEVEN

Undirected reading

Few pleasures, for the true reader, rival the pleasure of browsing unhurriedly among books: old books, new books, library books, one's own books, other people's books – it doesn't matter whose they are or where they are. Simply to be among books, glancing at one here, reading a page from one over there, enjoying them all as objects to be touched, looked at, even smelt, is a deep satisfaction. And often, very often, while browsing haphazardly, searching for nothing in particular, you pick up a volume that suddenly excites you, and you know that this one of all the others you *must* read. Those are great moments. And the books you come across like that are often memorable.

Bumping into books, as it were, has very little to do with other people and nothing at all to do with reviews or lists of set books, or seeing 'the film of the book' or publishers' publicity. Yet every reader knows how important it is as a way of coming across the books one most enjoys reading. And this is what leads me to wonder whether we do not try too hard to get children reading. We ought to trust books themselves more than we do. Too much talk about them can drive people away. And no matter how well we read aloud or do anything else to focus children's interest on particular books, unless they are given time to roam about un-hindered among books of many kinds, left alone to choose for themselves and to do just what any avid adult reader does, then maybe we labour in vain.

Letting children loose among a good stock of books to follow their own whims and fancies for half an hour or so every week is one of the cornerstones on which a permanent interest is built. It is, after all, pretty silly to get a horse thirsty and then never to let him near the pond to drink. And I sometimes think that teachers spend a lot of time on tasty stratagems that make their pupils thirsty for books but give them far too little time to quench that thirst not through prescribed texts but through those chosen from a catholic collection. It is a curious irony, when you consider it, that children are often allowed by teachers to read only what they are told to read, chosen from a library itself selected by the teachers!

Let us look at the advantages browsing offers.

Familiarity, first of all. People from 'non-book' homes feel that bookshops and big public libraries are alien places. All those shelves full of books are forbidding, daunting. Where do you start? Of course, once you get used to it, you develop a nose for sorting out what appeals to you. But there is no other way to get used to it than by doing it. Browsing time provided for in school, when there is a teacher that the children know well to help if necessary and when all their classmates are there too, is the only way many children will ever become familiar with books *en masse*. Left to themselves, they'll rarely pluck up courage to try. And this is the proper purpose of the library lesson.

Unfortunately, many teachers in the past have felt that library lessons should be used only to teach about the library, by which they meant instruction in how to use catalogues, and reference books and so on. Worse, others used the time for book-based project work, when the library was nothing but a book-filled classroom. As a result library lessons came into disrepute and even today authorities speak against them, arguing that the proper thing is for the library to be open to everyone at all times (which no one disagrees about) and for children to use it when they find it necessary, but that library lessons ought not to be specifically laid down in time-tables. What then happens is that only the avid readers browse in their own time; everyone else comes there only when sent by a teacher to look up a specific point or to get a book for some work in hand. Libraries, in short, become no more than resource centres, and books no more than tools. As I've said before, literature is not a tool.

But browsing is more than just a matter of familiarization with books for those who are not brought up with them. No true reader can be expected to grow on a diet of prescribed texts only, regardless of how well chosen they may be. No one can be completely successful in selecting books for someone else, no matter how well he know the other's tastes. Children, like the rest of us, need opportunities to seek out for themselves the books which will satisfy their immediate needs and suit their maturity of skill and personality. Browsing times offer that chance. Quite rightly teachers spend a lot of time suggesting books and trying to interest their pupils in them, but no more than a few in any group are ever attracted to what is shown them, and numerically the number of books that can be so presented is small.

Working individually with children is, of course, somewhat different; and this is another advantage that browsing offers. In these invaluable moments a teacher can try to get to know the needs and tastes of each child; he can talk informally about books he judges a child is ready for; he can encourage, stimulate and discuss in a manner which would be quite impossible in group situations. Just as importantly, he can leave a child alone to follow his own bent. The 'pace' of teaching can be geared specifically to a child instead of to a group whose members have disparate skills and requirements.

Nor is a teacher working alone during browsing times. In chapter six we have explored peer influences, and we must note again here the importance of the suggestions children make to each other; and while poking about among books they naturally discuss those they have read, swopping responses and so leading each other on. The teacher may have said nothing, but by providing the right setting and a relaxed discipline to protect the intention of the period, he has helped children to help themselves.

In schools that run their own bookshops (see chapter eight) browsing lessons can include buying as well as borrowing and returning books, adding another dimension of value to these times. On any one occasion there will always be pupils who do not want to borrow or buy, but they are still learning to live with books by bumping into them and by talking to each other about them.

Unsupported by any other teaching method, browsing is not, of course, enough to make children into literate readers. The idea that all we have to do is to surround children with books and everything else follows automatically is naïve. It would be enough for *some* but by no means *all*. On the other hand it is equally true that this kind of setting and activity is much more important than its casual, relaxed and unstructured nature makes it seem.

Undirected reading means more than browsing, however. It covers also what used to be called 'silent reading' when children are required to read to themselves uninterrupted a book of their own choice – though more often than not this means a book taken from a selection supplied from an approved list of 'set books'. At best, though, this follows on from browsing: a child chooses for himself from a large stock, and is then given time to read in class. When this is a regular provision throughout a child's school career, he gradually lays a solid foundation of skill and enjoyment on which directed reading – the close study of certain 'key' texts by a teacher and his class – must be built.

John Werner has briefly summarized the values of undirected reading thus:

1. Each pupil must be given the opportunity to read at his own speed material of a difficulty suited to him. Such reading requires frequent practice.

2. No teacher can estimate which book will satisfy the intellectual and emotional needs of the individual. Therefore many books must be tried.

3. Such reading cannot be left to the pupil's leisure time. Many children come from homes where serious reading is simply not part of

the way of life; T.V., with all its advantages, has surely cut down the incentive to acquire the habit of reading seriously where this is not already part of the accepted social pattern.

4. The teacher should not always be involved in the response to a book. Emotional blocks to reading can be formed by an unsatisfactory relationship with a teacher. With classes the size that they are it is not always possible for him to detect the problems soon enough. In any case, a previous teacher may have left him with the legacy of an un-satisfactory attitude to reading. Much 'free' writing in fact gives the teacher the response he wants. Response to teacher-dominated reading carries the same danger.

5. A teacher cannot keep up with all the books from which a child's reading should be selected. If directed reading is alone encouraged, the class will merely reflect the taste of the teacher rather than evolve their own.

6. If a child is reading only trash, then this fact should be taken into account and dealt with in English lessons. [See chapter ten, 'Worrying about the rubbish'.]

7. Many of our major authors (Dickens and Wells for example) were nourished on an early diet of wide, random reading, and in our own time, the number of outstanding young authors who are writing in spite of rather than because of classroom education is not incon-siderable. The outstanding example is Alan Sillitoe, who started writing seriously only after reading undisturbed during a lengthy spell in hospital.

8. The child must learn to discriminate for himself. If a pupil is allow-ed to accept or reject, he himself will demand higher standards in reading material far sooner than if his teacher attempts to tell him what is good and what is bad. (1. p. 162)

How should undirected reading lessons be conducted? What are the snags and problems? I have stressed, and Werner's summary emphasizes, that such lessons must be regular and frequent – at least one a week. But they cannot be imposed on children who are not used to them without some preparation. Essentially, they must be presented as pleasurable times to be looked forward to; and it is best if everyone comes prepared, knowing what they want to read. Classes which are not accustomed to the practice will need weaning: a good idea is to read aloud for a part of each lesson because this is a corporate activity that will settle them down and tune their imaginations to the right frequency; for the rest of the lesson they can be told to read their own books silently, and this part of the lesson can gradually be lengthened as the children grow in stamina and appetite.

In fact only very avid readers will ever settle to silent reading immediately on arrival from some different activity. A few minutes spent with teacher and pupils talking about books (new ones just in from the supplier, for example, or those people have read and want to recommend to others) or any book-related topic treated conversationally in a by-the-way fashion serves the double purpose of preparing the right set of mind while at the same time attracting attention to books that might be enjoyed. This is really a 'bridge passage' leading smoothly from one occupation – science, or P.E. or maths, etc. – to literary reading.

Younger and less skilled children are, of course, unable to sustain silent reading for very long, and younger children especially enjoy talking to themselves while they look at a book. But more mature readers can be expected to go on for full lessons without flagging, a point that most children should reach by late primary age. Others will need help in developing stamina and concentration by having rest times when what they are reading can be discussed; this gives them time to gether their energies again.

Once the silent reading practice is accepted then an understanding should also be reached that at these times classmates should not be interrupted, either for idle chatter or for sharing responses. This last is tricky. It is entirely natural for children to want to tell their pals about something they enjoy, and it is essential that this desire be given an outlet. If, however, it is allowed free play then the 'silent' reading is soon silent no longer, and whether children want to share their friends' reactions or not, they are disturbed by the noise of those who do. The most satisfactory answer to the difficulty is to make it a matter of routine that before the end of each session, time is allowed for swopping excitements, but that during the reading time these must be contained as a simple courtesy in recognition of other people's right to read undisturbed. Once established, a look, a nod, or a warning sign from the teacher is usually enough to remind forgetful children of the accepted mode of behaviour and to prevent distractions.

Reaching such a point of ease may be a long haul with some children and with classes who have unfavourable sets inbuilt from past bad teaching or lack of such experience; but this is the goal to be aimed for, and once attained it is a source from which other things flow: sessions of reading aloud to each other in small groups, and discussion or writing, drama or anthology programmes based on books read and in spontaneous response, begin to blur the line that seems, as I write of it here, to separate undirected reading from other activities. In practice, once the barriers are broken down in children antagonistic to reading, everything blends into the flux of a whole experience split into bits only by the dictates of a school time-table. The experience itself we can recognize is made up of:
1. selecting what to read;
2. the act of reading what has been selected;
3. expressing responses generated by the reading;

4. being thus led on to make further selections in order to enjoy the pleasure of reading again.

Clearly, browsing about to find one's own preferences and reading without intervention from others unless it is asked for are two major parts in that whole scheme. It is the teacher's job to make sure they are provided for in school.

References and further reading

1. John Werner, 'Undirected Reading' in Graham Owens and Michael Marland (eds.), *The Practice of English Teaching*, Blackie, 1970, p. 161. A collection of linked essays on English teaching in secondary schools, there are numerous hints and explanations of methods worth following up.
2. David Holbrook, *English for Maturity*, Cambridge University Press, 1961. The section titled 'Reading' (p. 150) has useful things to say about both directed and undirected reading in secondary schools.
3. Sybil Marshall and others, *Beginning with Books*, Basil Blackwell, 1971. Includes many examples of methods used by infant and primary school teachers to encourage avid reading.

EIGHT

Book buying: book owning

A relentless logic has turned many teachers into mini booksellers. Everything they know from theory and practice about the growth of literacy beyond a merely adequate minimum ability to obtain the simplest information and instruction points to the importance of book ownership as both a reflection of, and a formative influence on, a family's attitude to reading. What are called 'advantaged' homes, by which we mean those that offer their children the benefits every child should have, own their small libraries. But most children are, in this respect at least, disadvantaged: their homes possess few books, if any. At Christmas and on birthdays there might be some among the other presents, and if one of the family has a passionate interest in a hobby or pastime, a book, usually of the information kind, is found to satisfy his curiosity. But the idea of buying books as you buy clothes or groceries is an alien one.

Most parents are not like Prospero, who valued books above his dukedom, nor do they think as did Sydney Smith 'no furniture so charming as books'. They may genuinely want a better education for their children, and may often understand that reading lies at the heart of the matter. But because book ownership is something removed from their normal pattern of life, a pattern they grew up accepting, it is difficult to explain how strong is the connection between owning books and appreciating them fully, between buying books and reading them. After all, they argue, there are the so-called 'free' public libraries: self-service stores where you can go and get books without paying a new penny for them. So why pay good money just to own the things and have them collecting dust around the house? Against that kind of thinking it is pointless to quote research figures and surveys and reports about the factors that underlie the 'better education' everybody wants, reports like those written by Peter Mann at Sheffield University whose investigations of reading habits 'show the library users to be some way towards involvement in the world of books, but, on the whole, not as greatly involved as the people who use bookshops.'*

So teachers find themselves labouring against the grain. Educa-

* Peter H. Mann, *Books: Buyers and Borrowers*, Deutsch, 1971, p. 149 (see p. 3).

tional theory is based upon the assumption that the home environment complements the school; that it provides a background fertile for the child's educational development. Yet it is patently clear, so far as reading and books are concerned, that most homes play no such role. It is a theory built upon an assumption about a certain minority – those brought up in literate surroundings – and transferred as though it still held true on to a majority living under quite different circumstances.

What does a teacher do? Does he tackle the problem? Does he try by one method or another to awaken parents and children to the importance of owning books? Is such activity a proper part of a teacher's task; does it lie within the bounds of his responsibility? Ought he to spend time in this way? And how does he do it anyway?

Once an interplay between true literacy and book ownership has been convincingly established (and no one who thinks about it for two minutes and looks at the ever more numerous reports on reading and literacy can doubt that it has been) these questions must be answered. We find ourselves in a dilemma. Teachers are primarily charged with the education of children, but they are hindered in the discharge of their responsibility by an absence in the majority of homes of a cultural precondition that enables them to teach properly – and teach not only literature but everything else which depends on the printed word. They know what the precondition is; and they know that one aspect of it is the attitude to books in the home. Either they can labour on in the hope that someone else will do something about it, or they can do something about it themselves. And if they choose to do something themselves, they must readjust their thinking about educational methods and their responsibilities. They must be convinced that giving time to encourage children to buy books – indeed, giving time actually to sell books – is a directly educational activity. And they must consider that the education of parents lies legitimately within the bounds of their work.

Teachers who have seen that they must tackle the problem have on the whole managed to find ways of encouraging book buying. The task would have been easier (though probably less necessary, too) had bookshops been commonplace round the country, or indeed if booksellers had been as vigorous in their business as grocers and insurance agents in theirs. Good bookshops are few and far between; and the kind to be found in most towns, hybrid affairs dealing in newspapers, magazines, stationery, trinkets and a motley collection of paperbacks in cheap tin trays, is about as educationally healthy as a river rich in industrial effluent is physically salubrious. Opinions differ as to the best method for teachers to use. There are several, and which one to try depends somewhat on local circumstances *vis-à-vis* available bookshops, the organizing teacher's aims, and the extent to which the school authorities, in particular head teachers, are prepared to go.

The school bookshop

This is the most complete and permanent arrangement, and there are two systems on which it works. The first is the most usual. An agreement is made with a bookseller by which the school becomes an agency, a branch in effect, of his store. The bookseller is responsible for supplying the books, dealing with publishers, suppliers, and all financial matters. The school, through the organizing teacher, looks after the day-to-day management of the 'shop': fixing opening times, manning the counter, looking after the stock, informing the bookseller about orders and when fresh stock is needed, and accounting the money and sales. To make this system work well there must be close cooperation between school and bookseller; and the bookseller will, of course, look for some profit from his involvement, though it is likely to be very small. The school can expect no financial return but will know that there is expert help behind the venture and that it is released from any commercial entanglement.

The second system requires that the school seek a licence from the Publishers' Association to sell books, which, if granted, allows the school to operate as a bookshop in its own right, ordering directly from publishers and suppliers at the normal discount rates. The school bookshop is then a self-supporting business, with all this means in advantages and disadvantages. It is not a step to be taken lightly by anyone. The margins on bookselling are staggeringly small and the administrative complexities costly in time and effort. Certainly, before launching such an operation it is advisable to seek expert advice.

Within either system there is considerable variation in practice. Some schools run the very simplest of shops, no more than a portable cupboard containing a couple of hundred paperbacks which are put on sale once a week. Other schools elaborate. A table is set up in a classroom, books are laid out on it by pupil 'shop assistants' supervised by a rota of teachers, and regular opening hours are laid down and adhered to. Stock is stored in a cupboard when the shop is closed and some care is taken to advertise and promote sales. Nearer the ideal, there are schools which have managed to release an old room and convert it into a permanent, self-contained shop, an enterprise that needs enthusiasm from staff, pupils and parents. The ideal itself, attained by a few schools, is a specially designed bookshop built as part of the premises, properly sited, equipped with shelves, display space, counter, and all the correct fittings. The article *Penguin's Nest and After* reprinted as Appendix Four gives a graphic and useful account of the building of a bookshop in a school.

However rudimentary or advanced the system, and no matter what the age of the children involved, certain matters should be considered before setting out on the venture.

1. More than one member of staff ought to be directly in charge of the day-to-day organization. It is too much for one person to carry the load unaided. Furthermore, considerable sums of money must be properly handled; absence from school of the only organizer means that errors creep in very quickly, or that the shop has to be closed. And should the organizer leave altogether, the shop is likely to close for good. The whole value of a school owning its own bookshop lies in its permanence as a school institution and the continuing use of it by the children.

2. The responsibilities to be shared between the commercial bookseller, if there is one involved, and the school should be sorted out at the beginning. Whatever is agreed to, one thing should always be understood: that selection of stock is, in the end, the school's province. A good bookseller will know what sells well; but the school must, for its own protection, have the final say should disagreement arise in this area.

3. Teachers should not be the only ones to make decisions about stock on the school's behalf, however. Children have ideas to contribute and they should be listened to. They ought also to help to organize and run the business, just as pupils help in the library. This may be arranged through a bookshop committee; and in secondary schools there is no reason why a senior pupil cannot be appointed bookshop manager. Each class can also send in monthly suggestion lists after discussions in lesson time. Preparation of publicity posters, publication of the bookshop news-sheet: there are all kinds of ways that lead to participation by children.

4. For the most part, the stock will be made up of paperbacks: priced within the range of schoolchildren's pockets, they are also the format young people find most attractive. Experience will tell how many and which hardbacks to put on sale.

5. Even with the closest supervision some books will be lost through theft, a fact of life one must recognize and cope with. Temptation and opportunity should be kept to a minimum without at the same time imposing a restrictive and suspicious atmosphere on the proceedings. A good deal can be achieved in the right direction by careful planning during selling times: the room used should have only one door, and the cash desk should be placed by it. Each display point should be supervised by an assistant, either a pupil bookseller or a member of staff. Proper security during

closed times – locks on stock cupboards and a limit to the number of keyholders – is an obvious precaution.

6. Good publicity helps a school shop as it does any other. Opening times need plenty of announcement. Posters made by pupils to draw attention to the shop and to specific books; display boards for book jackets and publishers' material; the use of what the trade calls TV and film 'tie-in' promotion to channel topical interests; special occasions organized by the shop (visits by authors, book fairs and the like): all help to keep book buying in the children's minds. And at every school function where the shop can make a showing, it should be there, open for business: at school plays, parents' meetings, fêtes, open days, sports events.

7. In many teachers' experience a school bookshop begins with a rush of business which tails off after a few weeks. To some extent, this is something anyone might expect to happen, and it is not a sign of failure. On the other hand, the object is to sell books regularly to as many children as possible, and settling down with a steady clientele of kids who are readers anyway should satisfy no one. So the initial interest must be consolidated as quickly as possible; the first weeks are vital, and after that the shop must be constantly on the look-out for ways of stimulating further interest and re-awakening those who lapse. Gimmicky events are not very useful: they entertain for a while but do not put book buying and reading at the centre of attention. Less gawdy techniques are usually in the end more successful. 'Focus weeks', for instance, provide a boost in special directions, as when the shop puts on a show of sports books arranged perhaps in conjunction with a big match or sports event in the school. The chances are that children who are interested in the sport will come to the shop to see the show whether they are readers or not, and so make contact when otherwise they might not have done. What matters above all is the feeling of energy, of liveliness, of things going on: this is what will attract customers and keep them.

Unless a teacher is prepared to give thought to topics of this sort, and unless he is prepared to cope enthusiastically with an administrative responsibility that demands a lot in time, he had best not begin a bookshop at all. There are other methods of helping children to become book buyers which are less demanding and easier to operate.

Book fairs

These are bumper book sales arranged to suit the school's convenience, though three a year are the most that can be properly managed – one a term – and many schools who organize them find one or two enough (usually before the Christmas and summer holidays). Children, staff, parents, people from the neighbourhood are all invited to help, visit, join in the peripheral 'side-shows', and buy books. Once again careful planning pays dividends, and plenty of time and helpers are needed. There is now a wealth of experience gained by teachers who have organized fairs, and it is useful to talk to some who have taken part in them. A small fair lasting only a day, such as might be held in an infant school, can get by with a couple of members of staff and a parent as the organizing committee; but those held in big schools that last several days and are supported by exhibitions and linked activities require a commensurately larger collection of staff and children. In any case it is best to split up the work among all those involved, having an adult in charge of each 'department'. These are some of the main items to be considered:

1. TIME

A fair cannot be put on at a few days' notice. A decision has to be made at least two months before, allowing time to collect helpers, arrange for the supply of books, prepare publicity, make displays and exhibits, and fix up speakers. Book supply, for instance, can take six weeks, regardless of quantity.

The date for the fair often suggests itself, and, of course, must be fitted into the school programme so that it does not clash with any rival local or national event. Late November or early December is a good time because people have presents in mind for Christmas; a couple of weeks before spring and summer holidays helps to promote holiday reading. National, local and school celebrations like National Book Week, International Children's Book Day, centenaries of famous authors, founders' days, and the like provide focal dates.

The duration of the fair depends on many factors. A small country primary school can do in an afternoon and evening the same job for its community as a big city comprehensive will take at least two days and more likely a whole week to achieve. The aim is to provide enough time for every child and all parents to browse round and buy. This means that during the day groups of children look round the fair, and buy if they wish, or make lists of books they would like to have so that they can tell their parents what to buy for them. In the evenings and perhaps all day on a Saturday, the fair is open for visits from parents and friends as well as pupils. It is important that no one should be hustled through too quickly.

2. WHERE?

There should be plenty of space to lay out all the books attractively and for people to move about without feeling crowded. School halls make obvious sites; and large school libraries (if carefully prepared) are also suitable. If necessary more than one room can be used, but they should be close together, easily accessible and preferably on the ground floor. Large clear notices outside and inside the school should indicate what is being held and where. Car parking facilities will be needed and should be manned during the hours when it is open to the public. And toilet facilities should be available and well signposted.

3. BOOK SUPPLY

The easiest and most efficient method is to use a bookseller who provides all the books. He does not have to be near at hand, but there must be plenty of cooperation and consultation as to selection of stock. I give below a list of reputable booksellers who also claim to carry good stocks of children's books. Whichever bookseller is approached – and a number may have to be before one is found who is willing to help – it is a point of wisdom to assure oneself of his capabilities and the conditions he will impose before any arrangement is made.

A school can, of course, attempt to gather the books without the help of a bookseller, but this is exhausting and can be tricky unless the school already has a bookshop licence of its own and knows the ropes.

Scholastic Publications (see below) also help to set up fairs.

4. BOOK SELECTION

Whatever method of supply is used, it is essential that the school have some control over what is put on sale. But everyone must also realize that a fair is unlikely to be successful, commercially or otherwise, unless a broad selection of books is displayed. Certainly the school and public librarian, class teachers, and the children themselves can be consulted and their ideas taken account of, as well as the advice given by booksellers and suppliers who know which titles will be popular. Most schools favour paperback fairs for the reasons already given about cost and format. Each time a fair is held experience about selection will be gained, as well as about organization as a whole.

5. PUBLICITY

Very important, and the more the better. Teachers and children should know at least a month beforehand what is going to happen, and after the first announcement there should be a gradual build-up of anticipation by a planned programme of information about events and attractions. Publicity directed at parents and the neighbourhood should start going out from three weeks before the date.

Posters made by pupils can be got into local stores, banks, council offices, libraries, and anywhere else that people will allow. Also, of course, round the school.

Letters to parents announcing the fair and inviting them to visit it, giving dates, times, activities arranged are best sent through pupils about ten days before.

The local press will often take an interest, printing news 'stories' about the fair. Local radio too should be approached.

Groups like the Women's Institutes, Mothers' Unions, men's clubs and the like should be sent information.

6. LAYOUT

A decision has to be made about whether the books will be displayed higgledy-piggledy or according to a plan. Some schools favour subject arrangement, others group together everything by publisher, and others sort everything out according to a theme: there seems to be no consensus of opinion about what succeeds best. Whatever the plan, notices should help visitors to find their way among the books.

Always set the books out so that they show their fronts rather than their spines; and every copy should be within easy reach without others being knocked about.

Naturally people will handle books before they decide to buy them, which means that no more than a couple of copies of each title should be put out so that reserve stock is prevented from getting grubby. 'Assistants', each in charge of a section, will see that their bit is kept tidy and refurbished, while keeping an eye open for thieves.

Usually, tables are used on which to display the stock; decorated cardboard boxes placed on the tables help to vary the landscape and provide background. Shelves designed to hold front-facing books are naturally very useful if any are available.

7. SELLING POINTS

Restrict these to an efficient minimum – enough to cover exits from the rooms used. There should always be a responsible adult in charge, with a pupil assistant to put the bought books into paper bags and another to record sales by title and author, something that will be found useful not only in checking stock at the end of the fair but also in making decisions about selection for future events.

8. SIDE-SHOWS

Experience indicates that fairs which include additional attractions besides the 'core collection' of books sell more than those which do not. These can be as inventive as one cares to make them, but with one proviso: they should not be so diverting that they are visited for themselves alone. They should attract people into the sale, not from it. The following are some well-tried activities.

Talks by authors, illustrators, publishers. These should be well advertised and fixed for times when the largest audience can be expected. Expenses should always be paid and when possible a fee also. Many authors and special guests are glad to help in this way in the cause of book promotion, particularly when they live locally, but they should still be treated properly in the ways discussed in chapter nine, 'Star Performers'.

Story-telling and reading in a room set apart from the salerooms and led by competent people can either be an entertainment designed for all, or a way of solving the baby brother and sister problem. Parents can bring infant-school and primary-school children to a secondary-school fair and leave them in the story-telling room while they visit the sale. These sessions can be 'straight' or can involve recordings or film-strips.

Film shows. Short films like those made and loaned by Puffin Books about some of their authors exemplify what I mean by attracting to the sale, rather than detracting from it. Being short, they do not occupy visitors for too long, and being about well-known authors they may attract some people to buy their books.

Models and displays set up in the salerooms or as special exhibits are both decorative and interesting. They may comprise work done by pupils or hired from outside – things like the 'How a book is made' exhibition available from Brockhampton Press.

Plays and music performances in short programmes put on by staff and children at set times are always popular and require less arduous preparation than a full-length public performance. Scenes from books done in polished improvisations, for instance, or puppet plays adapted from stories are just right.

Refreshments prepared and served by PTA or staff and pupils during public opening hours are always welcomed by visitors and are often the only profit-making part of the occasion!

9. FOLLOW-UP

At the end of the sale, the main and least pleasant job is to sort out all remaining stock and check it against sales, as well as to dismantle display stands, exhibits, and publicity notices. When this is over, however, and everyone has had time to think, discussions should be held with helpers in which all details are gone over and suggestions made for improvements in the future. The school as a whole should also be given the chance to voice opinions and ideas, and class teachers should be encouraged to talk with their pupils about books they bought at the sale as a way of consolidating the work.

A book fair is a big occasion and ought to appear so. It should be colourfully presented and exciting to visit. As a means of encouraging the book-buying habit, however, it is useful only if regularly held at least once every school year. Ideally, fairs should lead to the introduction of a shop and should then be booster occasions helping to support children's buying habits.

Scholastic Publications

This is really a mail order firm operating through schools; it originated in the USA and claims to be firmly based on educational principles and guide-lines. Twice a term SP sends to each school taking part 'News sheets' which illustrate and describe a dozen or more books selected from ordinary paperback publishers' lists. Each child in the 'club' who wants to buy a book fills in an order form and gives it with his money to the organizing teacher who in turn makes up an overall order sheet and despatches it with a postal order to SP's warehouse. The books arrive for distribution ten days or more later. For pre-school children Scholastic run 'See-Saw Club', for infants 'Lucky Club', for 'junior level' 'Chip Club', and for secondary schools 'Scoop Club'. Books which might suit more than one 'level' may appear on two of the selections.

In the past Scholastic have provided a useful service, offering a fairly wide range of titles, both fictional and informational. The firm has recently lost key staff, however, and there must be some doubt about the direction in which it will go in future. The danger with it has always been that American books produced by the parent firm will be shipped to the UK and included in the selections to the detriment of British-published editions. Sample material should therefore be looked at before joining. The address is 161 Fulham Road, London SW3 6SW.

References and further reading

1. Penguin Education (School Bookshops), Penguin Books Ltd, Harmondsworth, Middlesex, offer to help and advise teachers setting up bookstalls and will send on request 'a list of points to observe'.
2. Marilyn Davies, 'The School Bookstall' in Graham Owens and Michael Marland (eds.), *The Practice of English Teaching*: Blackie, 1970, pp. 177.

Booksellers

The following list, arranged alphabetically according to towns, is not comprehensive, but gives booksellers understood to be children's book specialists. This does not, of course, mean they will all be willing to help with school bookshops. Make a careful investigation of stock and competence before entering into an arrangement with any bookseller.

ABERDEEN: A & R Milne & Wyllies, 247 Union Street.

ABERYSTWYTH: Siop y Pethe, Terrace Road. (Children's books in Welsh only.)
The Welsh Bookshop, Great Darkgate Street. (Children's books in Welsh only.)

ALTRINCHAM: Norman E. Lucas Ltd, 13 Ashley Road.

BANBURY: Children's Bookshop, 34 High Street.

BANGOR: Bookland, 40 Garth Road.

BANSTEAD: Ibis Bookshop, 109 High Street.

BATH: Bowes and Bowes (Cambridge) Ltd, 31 Milsom Street.
Tridias Ltd, 8 Saville Row.

BECKENHAM: Domino Children's Bookshop, 3 Village Way, High Street.

BEVERLEY: The Owl and the Beaver, 1 Wednesday Market.

BIRMINGHAM: Hudsons Bookshops Ltd, 116 New Street, 2.
Midland Educational Co., 104 Corporation Street.

BLACKBURN: Seed and Gabbutt, 40/42 Darwen Street.

BOGNOR REGIS: The Bookshop, 10 The Arcade.

BRAMHALL: The Bramhall Bookshop.

BRENTWOOD: Pied Piper, Hutton Road, Shenfield.

BRIGHTON: Bredon's Bookshop, 10 East Street.

BRISTOL: Clifton Bookshop, 84 Whiteladies Road, 8.
Pied Piper Bookshop, 65 Park Street, 1.
William George's Sons Ltd, 89 Park Street, 1.

BROMLEY: Hook's Bookshop, Westmoreland Place.

BROMSGROVE: Page One Bookshop, 3 Church Street.

CAMBRIDGE: Bowes and Bowes Ltd, 1/2 Trinity Street.
W. Heffer and Sons Ltd, 27 Trinity Street.

CANTERBURY: Pilgrim Bookshop, 29 St. Margaret's Street.

CARDIFF: Lear's Bookshop, 13-17 Royal Arcade.

CARLISLE: Charles Thurnam and Sons Ltd, 26-32 Lonsdale Street.

CARMARTHEN: C. Deryck Williams, 108 Lammas Street.

CHELTENHAM: Promenade Bookshop, 22 Promenade.

CHESTER: Bookland and Co. Ltd, Old Custom House Building, 70 Watergate Street.

CHICHESTER: Wessex Bookshop, 24 South Street.

CIRENCESTER: Paul Weller, 2 Dollar Street.

CROWBOROUGH: The Book Club, Croft Road.

DARTMOUTH: Harbour Bookshop, 12 Fairfax Place.
DERBY: Central Educational Co. Ltd, 36-38 St Peter's Churchyard.
DORCHESTER: Longmans, 4 Cornhill.
DUBLIN: A.P.C.K., 37 Dawson Street, 1.
Browne and Nolán Ltd, 56 Dawson Street, 2.
Easons, O'Connell Street, 1.
Hodges Figgis Co. Ltd, 5-6 Dawson Street, 2.
DUMFRIES: Blacklock, Farries and Sons Ltd, 17 Church Crescent.
EDINBURGH: The Edinburgh Bookshop, George Street.
James Thin, 52-59 South Bridge.
EXETER: J. F. Blackey Ltd, 10 Sidwell Street Shopping Centre.
FARNHAM: Hammick's Bookshop, Downing Street.
GLASGOW: W and R Holmes (Books) Ltd, 63 Buchanan Street, C1.
John Smith and Son (Glasgow) Ltd, 47-61 St Vincent Street, C2.
John B. Wylie and Co. Ltd, 406 Sauchiehall Street, C2.
GRIMSBY: A. Gait Ltd, 49 Friargate.
HALE: Johnstone's Bookshop.
HARROGATE: S. G. Hitchen Ltd, 14 Princes Street.
HATFIELD: The Hatfield Bookworm, 56 Town Centre.
HAVANT: Pelham Bookshop, 19 West Street.
HAYWARDS HEATH: Charles Clark Ltd, 19-21 Boltro Road.
HENLEY-ON-THAMES: The Bell Bookshop, 52 Bell Street.
HERTFORD: The Bookworm, 25 Parliament Square.
HORSHAM: The Bible Bookshop, 3 North Street.
HOVE: Combridge's (Hove) Ltd, 56 Church Road.
HULL: A. Brown and Sons Ltd, 24-28 George Street.
IPSWICH: The Deben Bookshop, The Ancient House.
KEW: Where the Wild Things Are, 9 Mortlake Terrace.
KNUTSFORD: G. Jardine Ltd, Old Market Place.
LANCASTER: Wigley's Bookshop, 69 Market Square.
LEEDS: Austick's Headrow Bookshop, 64 The Headrow.
LINCOLN: J. Ruddick Ltd, 287 High Street.
LIVERPOOL: Parry Books Ltd, 49 Hardman Street, 1.
Philip Son and Nephew, Ltd, 7 Whitechapel.
Charles Wilson (Booksellers) Ltd.
LONDON: Book One Ltd, 23 Temple Fortune Parade, Finchley Road, NW11.
Children's Book Centre Ltd, 140 Kensington Church Street, W8.
Don Gresswell Ltd, 9 Highgate High Street, N6.
(There are, of course, many others: see Telephone Directory.)
MAIDSTONE: County Town Bookshop, 57 High Street.
MANCHESTER: Sherratt and Hughes, 28-34 Cross Street.
W. H. Willshaw Ltd, 16 John Dalton Street, 2.
MARLBOROUGH: White Horse Bookshop, 136 High Street.
MILFORD HAVEN: The Fly Leaf, Robert Street.

NEWCASTLE UPON TYNE: Mawson, Swan and Morgan Ltd, Grey Street.

NORTHAMPTON: W. Mark & Co., 27 The Drapery.

NORWICH: Jarrold and Sons Ltd, 2-5 London Street.

NOTTINGHAM: Sisson and Parker Ltd, 25 Wheeler Gate, NG1 2NF.

OXFORD: B. H. Blackwell Ltd (Children's Bookshop), 22 Broad Street.

PAIGNTON: Children's Book Centre, 10 Crossways Shopping Centre.

PORTSMOUTH: The Portsmouth Bookshop, 14 Arundel Way.

PRESTON: Sweeten's Bookshops, 48 Fishergate.

RUGBY: George Over Ltd, 22 Market Place.

SEVENOAKS: The Sevenoaks Bookshop, 147 High Street.

SHEFFIELD: A. B. Ward, 35 Chapel Walk, Fargate, 1.

SHREWSBURY: Wilding & Son, 33 Castle Street.

SLOUGH: Carter and Wheeler Ltd, 280 High Street.

STROUD: Alan and Joan Tucker, The Children's Bookshop, Station Road.

SWANSEA: The Uplands Bookshop, 4 Gwydr Square.

TAUNTON: The Dragon Bookshop, The Crescent.
Pelican Bookshop, Magdalene Lane.

THAME: The Red House, Children's Bookshop, 42 High Street.

TWICKENHAM: Langton's Bookshop, 44 Church Street.

WALTON-ON-THAMES: Rainbow Bookshop, 27b Bridge Street.

WARWICK: John Gould, The Warwick Bookshop, 9 High Street.

WIMBLEDON: E. and W. Fielder Ltd, 54 Hill Road.

WINCHESTER: P. and G. Wells Ltd, 11 College Street.

WORTHING: Mason and Hodges Ltd, 6 Goring Road.

YEOVIL: Badgers Bookshop, 17 & 18 Bond Street.

YORK: Thomas C. Godfrey, Neville Duffield (Booksellers) Ltd, 21 and 25 Stonegate.

Further help and information

THE PUBLISHERS' ASSOCIATION: 19 Bedford Square, London W.C.1.

THE BOOKSELLERS' ASSOCIATION: 152 Buckingham Palace Road, London S.W.1.

THE NATIONAL BOOK LEAGUE: 7 Albemarle Street, London W.1.

THE SCHOOL LIBRARY ASSOCIATION: 150 Southampton Row, London WC1B 5AR.

THE EDUCATIONAL PUBLISHERS COUNCIL: 19 Bedford Square, London WC1B 3HJ.

THE ADVISORY CENTRE FOR EDUCATION: 32 Trumpington Street, Cambridge, CB2 1QY.

NINE

Star performers

My friends read my books not because they think I am any great shakes as a writer but simply because they know me. This is the only reason anyone needs for inviting authors in particular, out of all the professional book people, to meet children. Publicists – for good or ill – have learned their lesson: get an author on television to talk about himself and his work, and up go his sales; put him on the lecture circuit so that he meets people who often had never heard of him before he was introduced by the chairman, and the warehouse stock sheets graph his progress round the country. Profiles in newspapers and magazines, autograph-signing appearances in bookshops – any device at all that reveals the man behind the book does far more for an author's readership than yards of reviews or pages of expensive advertisements.

It is, surely, only natural. Children respond no less than adults (rather more, in fact) to personal contact. Popular authors receive scores, in some cases hundreds, of letters a year from their young readers (Malcolm Saville, for example, gets on average fifty a week); and every correspondent, I'm quite sure, wants a reply. Maybe they are all trying to answer the question a little girl once asked me: 'Do real people write books?' Real people do. And sometimes when you meet the 'reality' face to face you wonder how its owner ever managed to author anything and find yourself put off his books for life. But it is true nevertheless that by meeting authors (the plural is important) and asking them questions, talking about their books, doing things with them, children are drawn into a permanent involvement with literature. Cold print takes on a human voice; wadges of paper covered with words turn into treasured troves full of interest.

Authors-in-the-flesh bridge the gap between children and books in a fashion no one else can. Not because they have more skill than teachers or anyone else, but simply because they are authors: the people who created the books themselves. And it is always more interesting as well as enlightening to talk to the person who made the goods than to the person selling them.

We do not make enough use of writers and most of them, the children's writers especially, welcome opportunities to meet their audience. A writer's job is seldom glamorous, usually difficult and always lonely. A day away from it now and then, mixing with children, hearing their opinions, trying to answer their questions, can be an invigorating relief. And at worst, if the trip is a flop (it happens!), at least he is glad to get back to work. One should never hesitate to invite authors to visit children. But there are practical problems that need attention.

CHOICE

Choosing who to invite often decides itself. Children and teacher have, for instance, read a book and been especially excited by it. Asking the author to visit is a natural step to take. And it is even more obvious in the case of set books. Some authors, of course, object to their work being subjected to compulsory dissection for exams in the traditional deadly manner. Like Bernard Shaw, they swear to haunt anyone who so mistreats them (Shaw's ghost must be a busy spirit these days). Apart from this, some authors' books are very popular as set texts, and so they cannot possibly accept all requests or they would never write again. Discretion is needed, therefore. Recommendation by people who have seen them performing well with children – and not all have the gift – is another way of coming across authors worth inviting. A study topic in, say, history may suggest others. Then there are authors whose books are demanding: meeting them may well provide the stimulus some children need to read what they have written.

Over a period of time, two or three years, any one group of children should meet a mixture of writers: some whose books they know well and like, some who are new, some who produce information books, some who talk about their work and themselves, some who prefer to do things with the children. As time goes on and the list lengthens, the hope is that children will feel and respond to the infinite variety that books encompass. I am never quite sure what people mean when they speak of things being 'relevant'; but this sense of involvement, of living application and belonging is what I mean. And bringing writers of all kinds together with children helps everyone to discover that pertinent relationship.

MAKING THE APPROACH

When a private address is not known, authors are most easily reached through their publishers. The initial letter of invitation should include a stamped, self-addressed envelope and, to avoid unnecessary further correspondence, should provide at least the following details:

(i) Your own and/or the school's name, address, telephone number.

(ii) An outline of the reason why you are inviting the author to visit, what you would like him to do, the age and numbers of the children likely to be involved.

(iii) A selection of dates suitable to yourself, leaving the author free to choose the one most convenient.

(iv) The fee and expenses you can offer.

(v) The accommodation you can arrange should the visit require an overnight stay. (It is not always the case that visitors like to be houseguests of a family; they may prefer an hotel and should be given the option.)

(vi) The geographical position of the meeting place and its ease of access from major roads and railway stations. If transport from a railway station is needed, say whether you can provide it.

It is not wise, by the way, to make the first approach by telephone for this puts the author on the spot and he may refuse simply in self-defence – and especially if you happen to butt in when he is struggling with an obstinate chapter in a new book.

Given this kind of information a considered reply is possible and, because the invitation has been made in a business-like and considerate manner, the answer is more likely to be favourable.

Once the invitation has been accepted certain courtesies ought always to be extended:

(i) Because it is usually necessary to make the first approach well before the event, always confirm the arrangement nearer the date. In the same letter give final details about the visit, and provide, when wise to do so, a map of the vicinity of the meeting place.

(ii) Make sure that someone is responsible for greeting the visitor on arrival, seeing to his needs, and generally making him comfortable.

(iii) If the visitor is an author, illustrator, or publisher, some of his work should be on show.

(iv) Be sure any mechanical equipment required (tape machines, film projectors, etc.) does actually work, can be replaced at a moment's notice if it breaks down, and is handled by a competent operator.

(v) If there must be formal introductions and votes of thanks, at least see that what is said about the visitor is correct, that there are no lengthy public speeches that pre-empt the visitor's reason for being there at all, and that matters are kept as unembarrassing as possible.

(vi) Find out whether the visitor prefers to have the children on their own, or won't mind members of staff sitting in.

(vii) Make sure everyone – those involved and those who are not – is aware of time-table and room changes and any other administrative abnormalities; and as far as possible prevent any untoward interruptions. (I shall not quickly forget being halted in full flight during a visit to a college of education by the explosive entrance of a lecturer who, without pause for reflection or apology, set about an unfortunate student for not being at a tutorial. Apart from the fact that the lecturer was at fault for not attending to well-announced changes in programme, the incident did make one wonder about the way teachers are trained as well as about the nature of some of the people who teach teachers.)

(viii) When the visit is over send a letter of thanks: the gesture need not be merely an empty convention.

One would think it hardly necessary to give advice of this sort but harsh experience says otherwise. Anybody who has done a lot of talking in schools and colleges, at meetings in libraries and to professional as well as voluntary associations, has a fund of stories, hilarious in retrospect but which were irritating at the time, about the extraordinary treatment suffered at the hands of organizers. And there does seem to be a very close relationship between the size of the fee offered and the amount of care and thought taken; you learn to expect the worst when you are working for nothing.

MAKING THE MOST OF A VISIT
The 'star performer's' appearance ought to be only the high point of talking in schools and colleges, at meetings in libraries and to the visitor provides a focus and incentive. In preparation, it is fairly obvious that the children should be told about the coming visit well in advance and be made aware of the author and his work. Displays attract attention, and can include a photograph of the visitor and biographical details as well as any publicity material that might be available from publishers. All this is basic. What is more important perhaps is the effect that a prospective visit will have on the children's work activities; it will act as a stimulus, providing them with purpose and energy outside the usual run-of-the-mill work. A programme consisting of readings, improvised scenes, and scripted extracts from the author's work, or based on it, is the kind of major project I have in mind. Or adaptations might be made by children and recorded on tape in radio style. These would be performed shortly before the author's visit, or, of course, during it, for the benefit of all the children who will eventually meet him. In this way it is possible to bring together literary reading, script-writing, drama work of different kinds, craft work – illustrations for scenes in the books, models for displays, posters about the visit, decorations for the room where it is to take place – and, of course, plenty of talk as plans are made, and the work discussed and argued about. All this has tremendous educational value. I remember with great pleasure, for instance, a class of second-year 'backward' secondary-school

pupils putting on a puppet show they had written and performed for me after seeing their school's production of one of my plays. The puppet play was loosely based on the ideas in mine, but only loosely. The puppets were simple creations: cardboard heads painted and stitched onto pieces of cloth which formed the glove. The theatre was made of three draped art-room tables. The script was improvised on an outline which, I gathered, was the result of three lessons' hard talking to decide whose ideas out of the many suggested should be used. The production itself lasted half an hour (at least twice as long as it had ever taken in any of the numerous rehearsals!) and was vastly entertaining throughout. Of one thing I am certain: nothing I could have done for or with those children would have been half so valuable as all they did for themselves, with their teacher to fall back on when necessary. My only use was as a catalyst, an agent which the teacher could introduce into his everyday work as a way of adding something extra that gave intensity and excitement. And I was happy to be of that little use. Just by being a stranger who was also that odd fish, a 'writer', I had helped to create a context in which the reading those children had to do in preparing their play, the writing, the concentrated talking, the play rehearsing in breaks and after school as well as in lesson time, and the final production itself were no longer school exercises imposed, in their eyes, with little reason and less fun.

What is absolutely certain is that without some preparation by the teacher, a visitor cannot hope to achieve very much; he is in little better a position than cold fish on a marble slab. There is no strong interest for him to build on and he has to start by creating interest. Which brings me to the visit itself. It should not be assumed that this has got to be a semi-formal talk, followed by a few half-hearted questions: a kind of Queen's visit to the barracks. The guest might be better employed seeing small groups – half a dozen or so – at a time for quarter of an hour, when they could chat about anything that crops up. Where there have been elaborate preliminary projects, it may be better to centre everything on these. Or the author may prefer to base everything on his work, reading from it and discussing with the children. Whatever is decided upon, it seems to me a mistake not to allow time and opportunity for children to meet the visitor on their own. Too often guests are snatched up on arrival and closeted away from the children before being produced like a rabbit out of a hat for the 'official' appearance, which is no sooner over than they are hustled off once again, out of reach of anyone but members of staff or the organizer's chosen associates. No doubt this is done out of consideration for the visitor, and going into a school as a 'star performer' is certainly a strain. But it is the value of these occasions that we are looking for, and if one takes on such a job one expects to work hard. It is far better, it seems to me, to pay a visitor well and arrange plenty for him to do, than to pay him badly and be satisfied with a few minutes' talk. Exactly how much time should be spent letting children meet the visitor informally and how this might best be arranged is something to be discussed before the event.

Finally, out of sight should not mean out of mind. True, a visit may have been so disastrous that it is best forgotten; but this is not usually the case. Most 'star performers' leave behind some new interest that ought to be nurtured and strengthened. And this throws up lines of approach. Those children whose appetites were whetted need to be sought out and the books they want made available. (A point that might be anticipated: stocks could be bought in before the visit ready for this moment.) Some lesson time should be given up to discussing the visit, answering questions left unanswered and generally consolidating the experience.

PAYMENT

Local authority fees paid to visiting speakers are no less than insulting. Based, as they seem to be, on some kind of time-on-the-job calculation, they take into account neither the professional worth nor the practical realities of the work. Frequently, even this pittance is refused to teachers wanting to pay an author for a school visit, because it does not fit in with some spurious bureaucratic regulation. The trouble lies in the rigidity of a single basic fee. A one-hour session by an author in a local school costs him in time and effort far less than a full day spent in a school miles from home. Even an unintelligent council clerk can appreciate that the same fee paid for both jobs is neither just nor practicable. But that is what tends to be the rule. Similarly, it is naïve to suppose that the same fee for the same work can be offered to an established literary figure much in demand and an emergent writer whom a teacher has happened upon by accident. There should be flexibility in fees, some room for negotiation between teacher and visitor. And there should also be a far more realistic basic scale. Despite the antediluvian and dictatorial conditions imposed by many LEAs on those they charge with the responsibility for teaching children, there are ways of adjusting payment to suit the occasion and the speaker.

The most obvious is to obtain the LEA fee and to add to it out of school discretionary funds.

Secondly, the visit can be so organized that two fees are paid for the one trip. The author visits the school during, say, the afternoon for the LEA fee, and in the evening speaks to a local SLA, NATE, PTA, or other body (most of whom are short of money too), collecting his fee for this. The visitor thus spends his time efficiently and for a more reasonable financial reward, apart from the other obvious advantages all round. But you need a sympathetic visitor to do all this!

Thirdly, the author can be chosen from the Arts Council's list of approved 'Writers in Schools'. (Details from local LEA offices who are supposed to have the appropriate Department of Education memorandum; or direct from the Arts Council.) This works as follows. A writer selected from the Arts Council list agrees to make a visit; the organizing authority informs the Arts Council Director of Literature not later than one month before the date fixed. Afterwards, the author is paid his fee and expenses, and the Arts Council is billed for reimbursement of half the fee not later than two months after the visit.

The Arts Council suggest at present a basic fee of £20 for a one-day visit to a single institution; more if the author's stature warrants negotiation. This is adequate. The rub is that the Council's list of writers is by no means comprehensive. A committee of unnamed people selects the writers, revising the list every so often, but as far as I can gather it is a law unto itself and will only consider recommendations, no more. Nevertheless, the instrument is there and ought to be used as often as possible. Added to which the Arts Council rate of payment establishes a guide-line on fees that should be brought to the notice of local authorities every time a request for a 'star performer' is put in. £20 may seem a well-padded amount for a day's work. But it must be remembered that a one-day visit involves an author in travelling to and from the event, time spent preparing what is to be done, time afterwards reorientating himself to the very different business of writing. It is always hard to convince people that disruption of a writer's habits and rhythm of work has, for most of them, unsettling repercussions that upset his progress quite disproportionately to the actual time taken by the visit.

On the other hand it must also be re-emphasized that when a writer *is* being adequately paid for his services then he should be employed to full advantage *to the children*. Trotting along for an hour lecture to a group large or small does not, it seems to me, constitute a day's work. More should be given and more expected than that.

Throughout this chapter I have spoken of authors making visits. But other people can be as effective. Authors seem to have the most curiosity value, that's all! Publishers have much to offer children, and librarians, booksellers, printers all have obvious parts to play in widening the appeal of books and children's knowledge and appreciation of them. Perhaps what they all do more importantly than anything else is to remove the burden from the teachers' shoulders. By seeing and meeting all kinds of people who are involved with the printed word children come to realize that books are more than schoolroom tools, and that they satisfy many needs and provide many pleasures.

References

The Director of Literature, The Arts Council of Great Britain, 105 Piccadilly, London W1V OAU.
People in Wales should write to: The Welsh Arts Council, Holst House, Museum Place, Cardiff CF1 3NX.
The relevant document is 'Writers in Schools'.
Publishers' addresses, when not given in one of their books, can be obtained from either:
Antony Kamm and Boswell Taylor, *Books and the Teacher*, University of London Press;
or: *The Writers' and Artists' Year Book*, A. and C. Black.
Authors' addresses can often be found in:
The Author's and Writer's Who's Who, Burke's Peerage.

TEN

Worrying about the rubbish

By 'rubbish' adults usually mean literature which in their judgement lacks any artistic, moral or educational value. And the objection to it seems to be that by reading rubbish children cripple their own imaginative, linguistic and moral powers, as well as their ability to come to grips with and appreciate good quality literature. Whatever the objections may be, one thing is sure: teachers and librarians worry about the rubbish children read. Their worries are not altogether unfounded but they are sometimes carried too far. No one would suggest that children should be encouraged to read rubbish – they do not need encouragement on that score – but some people would suggest that they should be strongly *discouraged*, and then, I believe, more harm than good is done. Let me try and give my reasons.

First of all, Dr Johnson's well-known dictum comes to my aid: 'I would let [a child] first read *any* English book which happens to engage his attention; because you have done a great deal when you have brought him to have entertainment from a book. He'll get better books afterwards.'* This matches up with what Helen Gardner says in the passage quoted earlier where she recommends that the young need on the one hand 'to be encouraged to read for themselves, widely, voraciously, and indiscriminately ...'† The teacher's job is to lead on, to help children read 'with more enjoyment and understanding what [they] have found to be of value.' But this is not done by restriction, suppression or a snooty dismissal of the 'rubbish' that children happen to like. Even when a child seems to be reading nothing else but rubbish, at least we know that he is reading something: he still has a finger-hold on the written word, and we still have a hope of widening his range and vision. In the end, it is always better that children read something than that they read nothing at all.

But the problem is not usually so extreme. When children read at all they usually read more than a diet of rubbish only. (The only really worrying problem is when they read nothing.) And this introduces a second point. I am not convinced that people become 'fans' or even connoisseurs – experts, educated and discriminating people in any sphere – from limited knowledge and

* Quoted in Boswell, the *Life of Johnson* for 1779.
† See p. 30 above.

experience, no matter how rich and puristic in quality. On the contrary, they are connoisseurs because they know their subject inside out: the good, bad and indifferent. Wide, voracious, indiscriminate reading is the base soil from which discrimination and taste eventually grow. Indeed, if those of us who are avid and committed readers examine our reading history during our childhood and look also at what we have read over the last few months, few if any of us will be able to say honestly that we have always lived only on the high peaks of literature. Nor would we have it any different. The sum total of the pleasure we have had from books owes something to the ephemeral, transitory material we have frequently read. There is no reason why we should think that what is true for ourselves will be any the less true in this respect for other people – children or adults.

Both the points I have made so far can be summed up in one: that children must be allowed to discover for themselves. In the chapter on browsing and undirected reading I emphasized the fact known to us all that the books we come across by accident for ourselves often seem charged with greater attraction than those we are led to by other people. Inevitably, a large proportion of these self-chosen books will be slight in literary stature. But this is not what matters. The important thing is that by finding books in this unimposed manner we learn, however crudely at first, to compare, assess, select. There is no way this can be taught without direct, if haphazard, experience.

A third point, and one that harks back to the chapter on peer influences. Children have a group, social life; they belong to a clan of friends. And like any group, any clan, a company of children is cemented together by shared interests, which we frequently recognize as 'crazes'. For a time a gang of boys may be consumed by an interest in certain comics, or for Biggles books, or for motorcycle magazines, just as girls fall in love with pony books or stories about actresses or teenage romance magazines. A parent or teacher who attempts to deny this kind of rubbish to a child is attacking the child's feeling of group identity, of belonging. And there is no sense in doing that; by imposing a ban one is only likely to set up antagonism and frustration which will turn against the very thing we are trying to encourage. This is not to say we should pay no attention to the reading children do as part of their group alliances. On the contrary. We can discover a lot from knowing about it; it can help us to decide how to approach our teaching: the books we select and the techniques used to introduce and study them. Furthermore, children can be misled by group influences into reading truly pernicious material (hard core pornography, for example) and when this happens adults have a clear responsibility to step in and do something about it. But I'm not discussing pernicious material here; rubbish is neither pernicious nor particularly enlightening; it is merely absent of literary quality. But even if I were to bring this aspect into view I hope we would want to agree that the way *not* to handle the problem is by a ham-fisted act of unreasoned censorship exercised with deaf authoritarian zeal.

Reading crazes pass through groups of children like emetics, just as crazes for certain seasonal pastimes do. The interest is not really in the craze itself but in the intense socially binding effect it has on the individuals in the group. What remains afterwards for the participants as individuals is a more or less (depending on the child) increased facility in the imaginative, mental or physical skills involved. Thus in games, manipulatory skills are often exercised and extended, as for example in games that involve running, tree-climbing or making objects – bows and arrows, catapults, clothes for dolls, and so on. In reading crazes a child is exercising at the very least his ability to read; his reading muscles are limbered. And this is not to be dismissed lightly because it is an essential part of everyone's development as a reader. What's more, when a number of children read the same book with the kind of intensity they do during a craze, they talk and argue about it with equal intensity and so are forced to explore their individual and group responses, to formulate and articulate their enjoyment or dislike. They become involved, in other words, in criticism. In the beginning it does not matter what kind of literature causes this to happen; the great thing is that the critical sense has been awakened.

We're drawn back again – and this is the fourth thread in my argument – to my earlier assertion that what should concern us most is how and why children read, not what they read. I am not at all persuaded that children read everything in the same way, any more than adults do. Just the opposite. It has been frequently noted by writers on this subject that all children seem to find a source of security and comfort in certain kinds of books. Usually these are books which are very familiar to them, or by a writer of whom they are fond. At other times they may be doing nothing else but relax: passing the time in a pleasant if untaxing recreation. More often than not books chosen for this kind of reading are, in adult eyes, rubbish. But to tamper at such times by trying to persuade the child to choose 'something better' neither cures the cause nor encourages an improvement in standards of choice.

It is very difficult at any time to discover exactly what a child is taking from a book; it may, in fact, be something very different from anything the adult mind supposes the book does or does not offer. Let me try to suggest an example by instancing the much condemned Enid Blyton, an author whose work is criticized for its triviality, linguistically impoverished style, anaemia in plot and characterization, and clichéd, stereotyped ideas. I suspect that this very absence of quality is what makes Blyton so attractive to children, not because she is easy to read, undemanding, untaxing imaginatively and verbally but because her simplistic plots, her basic, undecorated, clichéd language and characters leave children free to embroider and enrich her stories *in their own way*. Blyton provides an outline; the young reader uses the outline on which to graft his own refinements. The more resourceful the literature, whether it be a great classic or pernicious pornography, the less it can be read in this way. You cannot, for example, read William Mayne in such a fashion; he is too demanding – you have to give yourself up to him, resting in him while he transports you through a very fully realized and detailed story. In terms of literary criticism Mayne will come out best over Blyton; comparison only throws into greater relief his qualities and her inadequacies (as well, let it be said, as her considerable talent as a 'what-happens-next' plot-maker). From the point of view of literary reading Mayne is respectable, Blyton is not. But my whole point is that in reading Blyton children are not engaging in literary reading. Anyone who has taught drama knows how children like to be given an outline to set them off on improvised drama-play. Having got started they then invent for themselves, turning the original outline into something quite different and completely their own. I believe they sometimes use books in the same way for interior, imaginal improvisation. Offer Blyton or Mayne for this purpose and Blyton is acceptable, Mayne certainly is not. I am not suggesting children do this every time they read a book. But they do read like this often and, I think, need to just as much as they need outward play.

There is an interesting experiment for testing this supposition. Think of a book which gave you great pleasure as a child but which you haven't read since. Remark every detail that you can remember. Then find a copy and reread it. The surprising thing to me when I tried the experiment was that many of the details I could remember were not in fact in the text at all. What is more, the text itself – with some notable exceptions – was unbelievably 'thin'. The non-existent details were, I presume, my own inventions, and the remembered fullness of the text a creation of my own reworking of the original 'outline' or 'script'. The notable exceptions I mention are, of course, the great books, and the reverse is true about these. I remember less about them than, on every rereading, I discover they possess. The great books always have something new to reveal. *The Wind in the Willows* is, for me, in this category, for example, while *Mr Bumbletoes of Bimbleton*, the book I used for my experiment (now regrettably out of print, and, for most people no doubt, out of mind), is in the category of 'interior play scripts'.

What we are discussing then is two ways of reading: the literary and the non-literary referred to in chapter one. And it is pointless to argue whether one is *the* essential way of reading and the other something to be suppressed, if it is true, as I suggest, that children need both. They are not in opposition, as people think when they worry about rubbish. All that has to be said is that once children start reading they will find their own non-literary material without wanting help from teachers; whereas to become literary readers they do need help.

One last thought. How often have we actually read what we condemn as rubbish? And how sure are we that it is rubbish after all? Peter Dickinson in an article 'A Defence of Rubbish' expressed what I have in mind:

> The adult eye is not necessarily a perfect instrument for discerning certain sorts of values. Elements – and this particularly applies to science fiction . . . – may be so obviously rubbishy that one is tempted to dismiss the whole product as rubbish. But among those elements there may be something new and strange to which one is not accustomed, and which one may not be able to assimilate oneself, as an adult, because of the sheer awfulness of the rest of the stuff; but the innocence – I suppose there is no other word – of the child's eye can take or leave in a way that I feel an adult cannot, and can acquire valuable stimuli from things which appear otherwise overgrown with a mass of weeds and nonsense. (1. p. 9)

Worrying about the rubbish is a fruitless business. The time and energy is much better spent bringing children into touch with the whole body of their rich literary inheritance.

References and further reading

1. Peter Dickinson, 'A Defence of Rubbish' in *Children's Literature in Education*, No 3, November 1970, Ward Lock Educational, p. 7. A well-argued case, based on a talk given to a conference on children's literature.
2. For more discussion of Enid Blyton see 'The Work of Enid Blyton' by Janice Dohm in *Young Writers Young Readers*, Boris Ford (ed.), Hutchinson, rev. ed., 1963; and comments in Wallace Hildick, *Children and Fiction*, Evans, 1970.

List of books
and sources of information

This short list is not exhaustive, but includes books and sources of information I have found useful either in writing this volume or in my own teaching. Some items fall easily into categories but others have been less tractable and these I have collected under the 'Miscellaneous' heading.

Bibliographical sources

Marcus Crouch (ed.), *Books about Children's Literature*, Library Association, rev. ed., 1966.

Virginia Haviland (ed.), *Children's Literature: A Guide to Reference Sources*, Washington, USA, Library of Congress, 1966. *First Supplement*, 1972.

Histories of children's books

Marcus Crouch, *Treasure Seekers and Borrowers: Children's Books in Britain, 1900–1960*, Library Association, 1962.

Harvey F. J. Darton, *Children's Books in England: Five Centuries of Social Life*, Cambridge University Press, 2nd ed., 1958.

Frank Eyre, *British Children's Books in the Twentieth Century*, Longman, rev. ed., 1971.

Roger Lancelyn Green, *Tellers of Tales*, Edmund Ward, rewritten and rev. ed., 1965.

Bettina Hürlimann, *Picture-book World*, Oxford University Press, 1968.

Bettina Hürlimann, *Three Centuries of Children's Books in Europe*, Oxford University Press, 1967.

Lee Kingman and others, *Illustrators of Children's Books 1957–1966*, The Horn Book, Boston, USA, 1968.

Bertha E. Mahony, *Illustrators of Children's Books 1744–1945*, The Horn Book, Boston, USA, 1947.

Cornelia Meigs and others, *A Critical History of Children's Literature*, Macmillan of New York, USA, rev. ed., 1969.

Percy H. Muir, *English Children's Books 1600–1900*, Batsford, 1954.

Mary F. Thwaite, *From Primer to Pleasure*, Library Association, 1963.

John Rowe Townsend, *Written for Children: An Outline of English Children's Literature*, Garnet Miller, 1965.

Ruth Hill Viguers and others, *Illustrators of Children's Books 1946–1956*, The Horn Book, Boston, USA, 1958.

Criticism

Eleanor Cameron, *The Green and Burning Tree: On the Writing and Enjoyment of Children's Books*, Atlantic-Little, Brown, Boston, USA, 1969.

David Daiches, *Critical Approaches to Literature*, Longman, 1964.

Sheila Egoff and others, *Only Connect: Readings on Children's Literature*, Oxford University Press, 1969.

Helen Gardner, *The Business of Criticism*, Oxford University Press, 1959.

Wallace Hildick, *Children and Fiction*, Evans, 1970.

Richard Hoggart, *Speaking to Each Other*, Vol. Two: *About Literature*, Chatto and Windus, 1970.

C. S. Lewis, *An Experiment in Criticism*, Cambridge University Press, 1961.

I. A. Richards, *Principles of Literary Criticism*, Routledge and Kegan Paul, reset ed., 1967.

Lillian Smith, *Unreluctant Years: A Critical Approach to Children's Literature*, The Viking Press, New York, USA, paperback ed., 1967.

J. R. R. Tolkien, *Tree and Leaf*, Allen and Unwin, 1964.

John Rowe Townsend, *A Sense of Story: Essays on Contemporary Writers for Children*, Longman, 1971.

Geoffrey Trease, *Tales Out of School*, Heinemann Educational Books, 2nd ed., 1964.

Surveys

Marcus Crouch, *The Nesbit Tradition: The Children's Novel 1945–1970*, Ernest Benn, 1972.

Margery Fisher, *Intent Upon Reading: A Critical Appraisal of Modern Fiction for Children*, Brockhampton Press, 2nd ed., 1964.

Margery Fisher, *Matters of Fact: Aspects of Non-fiction for Children*, Brockhampton Press, 1972.

Muriel Lock and others, *Reference Material for Young People*, Clive Bingley, rev. and enlarged ed., 1971.

Sheila Ray, *Children's Fiction: A Handbook for Librarians*, Brockhampton Press, rev. ed., 1972.

Lists of books for children and young people

Brian Alderson, *Reading for Enjoyment for 6–8 year olds*, Children's Booknews, 1970.

Centre for the Teaching of Reading, *Learning to Read: A Catalogue of Books for All Ages and Stages*, C.T.R., 1972.

Aidan Chambers, *Reading for Enjoyment for 12 year olds and up*: Children's Booknews, 1970.

Kenneth Charlton, *Recent Historical Fiction for Secondary School Children*, The Historical Association, rev. and rewritten, 1969.

Eileen Colwell and others, *First Choice: A Basic Book List for Children*, Library Association, 1969.

Judith Elkin (ed.), *Books for the Multi-racial Classroom*, Library Association Youth Libraries Group, 1971.

Anna Evillen, *Books for Dyslexic Children*, North Surrey Dyslexic Society, 1970.

J. A. Hart and J. A. Richardson, *Books for the Retarded Reader*, Ernest Benn, 1971.

Peggy Heeks, *Books of Reference for School Libraries*, School Library Association, 2nd ed., 1968.

Janet Hill and others, *Books for Children: The Homelands of Immigrants in Britain*, Institute of Race Relations, 1971.

Jessica Jenkins, *Reading for Enjoyment for 9 to 11 year olds*, Children's Booknews, 1970.

Mary Junor, *Stories to Tell*, Library Association Youth Libraries Group, 1968.

Kathleen Lines, *Four to Fourteen*, Cambridge University Press, 2nd ed., 1956.

Margaret Meek (ed.), *Puffins and Primary Schools*, Penguin Books, 1972.

Elaine Moss, *Children's Books of the Year*, Hamish Hamilton, 1970 onwards annually.

Elaine Moss, *Reading for Enjoyment for 2 to 5 year olds*, Children's Booknews, 1970.

National Book League, *Guide to Touring Exhibitions and Booklists*: National Book League, 1972.

Look for especially: *Fiction for the Middle School*, 1971; *School Library Non-fiction*, 1970; *Help in Reading*, 1968 (*Supplement*, 1970).

Sheila and Colin Ray, *Attitudes and Adventure*, Library Association Youth Libraries Group, 3rd ed., 1971.

School Library Association, *Books for Primary Children*, School Library Association.

C. A. Waite (ed.), *Periodicals for Schools*, School Library Association, 1969.

Books of use to the teacher and his work

Connie Alderson, *Magazines Teenagers Read*, Pergamon, 1968.

May Hill Arbuthnot, *Children and Books*, Scott, Foresman, Chicago, USA, 3rd ed., 1964.

Sydney Bolt and Roger Gard, *Teaching Fiction in Schools*, Hutchinson Educational, 1970.

James Britton, *Language and Learning*, Allen Lane The Penguin Press, 1970.

Kenyon Calthrop, *Reading Together: An Investigation into the Use of the Class Reader*, Heinemann Educational Books, 1971.

Joan Cass, *Literature and the Young Child*, Longman, 1967.

Aidan Chambers, *The Reluctant Reader*, Pergamon, 1969.

Kornei Chukovsky, *From Two to Five*, University of California Press, 1968 (and available in UK from Cambridge University Press).

Elizabeth Cook, *The Ordinary and the Fabulous*, Cambridge University Press, 1969.

Robert Druce, *The Eye of Innocence: Children and their Poetry*, University of London Press, 2nd ed., 1970.

Daniel Fader, *Hooked on Books*, Pergamon, 1968.

David Holbrook, *English for Maturity*, Cambridge University Press, 1961.

Anthony Jones and June Buttrey, *Children and Stories*, Basil Blackwell, 1970.

Antony Kamm and Boswell Taylor, *Books and the Teacher*, University of London Press, 2nd ed., 1970.

Sybil Marshall and others, *Beginning with Books*, Basil Blackwell, 1971.

Eric Newton and Graham Handley, *A Guide to Teaching Poetry*, University of London Press, 1971.

Graham Owens and Michael Marland (eds.), *The Practice of English Teaching*, Blackie, 1970.

Ernest Roe, *Teachers, Librarians and Children: A Study of Libraries in Education*, Crosby Lockwood, 1965.

George Sampson, *English for the English*, Cambridge University Press, new ed., 1952.

Robin Skelton, *The Practice of Poetry*, Heinemann Educational Books, 1971.

Journals and magazines

(a) REVIEW SOURCES
Books For Your Children (1965 . . .), 4 p.a.
   The Editor, 14 Stoke Road, Guildford, Surrey.

Children's Book Review (1971 . . .), 6 p.a.
The Editor, Five Owls Press, 67 High Road, Wormley, Brox-
bourne, Herts.
Growing Point (1962 . . .), 9 p.a.
The Editor, Ashton Manor, Northampton, NN7 2JL.
The Horn Book Magazine (1924 . . .), 6 p.a.
The Editor, 585 Boylston Street, Boston, Mass. 02116, USA.
Junior Bookshelf (1936 . . .), 6 p.a.
The Editor, Marsh Hall, Thurstonland, Huddersfield.
The School Librarian (1937 . . .), 4 p.a.
The Editor, The School Library Association, 150 Southampton
Row, London WC1B 5AR.
The following newspapers and journals carry regular reviews:
*The Times Literary Supplement, The Times Educational Supple-
ment, Teachers World, The Teacher, The Guardian, The Times,
The Listener, The New Statesman, The Spectator, New Society,
The Sunday Times, The Observer.*

(b) CRITICISM
Children's Literature in Education (1970 . . .), 3 p.a.
The Editor, 23 Ashlone Road, London SW15 1LS.
Signal (1970 . . .), 3 p.a.
The Editor, The Thimble Press, Weaver's, Amberley, Glos
GL5 5BA.

(c) JOURNALS DEVOTED TO THE TEACHING OF
     ENGLISH
English in Education (1966 . . .), 3 p.a.
William Spouge, 5 Imperial Road, Edgerton, Huddersfield
HO3 3AF.
The Use of English (1949 . . .) 4 p.a.
Scottish Academic Press, 25 Perth Street, Edinburgh EH3 5DW

(d) FOR CHILDREN
Puffin Post (1967 . . .) 4 p.a.
The Editor, Penguin Books, Harmondsworth, Middlesex.

Miscellaneous

Peter Coveney, *The Image of Childhood*, Penguin Books, 1967.
Brian Doyle, *The Who's Who of Children's Literature*, Hugh Evelyn,
1968.
Paul Hazard, *Books, Children and Men*, The Horn Book, Boston,
USA, 1944.
Janet Hill, *Children Are People*, Hamish Hamilton, 1973.

Richard Hoggart, *The Uses of Literacy*, Chatto and Windus, 1957; Penguin Books, 1958.

Peter H. Mann and Jacqueline L. Burgoyne, *Books and Reading*, André Deutsch, 1969.

Peter H. Mann, *Books: Buyers and Borrowers*, André Deutsch, 1971.

Iona and Peter Opie, *The Lore and Language of Schoolchildren*, Oxford University Press, 1959.

Iona and Peter Opie, *The Oxford Book of Nursery Rhymes*, Oxford, The Clarendon Press, 1955.

Levin L. Schücking, *The Sociology of Literary Taste*, Routledge and Kegan Paul, 2nd ed., 1966.

William Walsh, *The Use of Imagination: Educational Thought and the Literary Mind*, Chatto and Windus, 1959; Penguin Books, 1966.

Appendices

Readings that relate to some aspects of the text

ONE: Relating to Chapter One

WHY I VALUE LITERATURE
by Richard Hoggart*

I value literature because of the way – the peculiar way – in which it explores, re-creates and seeks for the meanings in human experience; because it explores the diversity, complexity and strangeness of that experience (of individual men or of men in groups or of men in relation to the natural world); because it re-creates the texture of that experience; and because it pursues its explorations with a disinterested passion (not wooing nor apologizing nor bullying). I value literature because in it men look at life with all the vulnerability, honesty, and penetration they can command ... and dramatize their insights by means of a unique relationship with language and form.

'Exploring human experience' is a useful phrase, but not quite sufficient. It is too active. 'Contemplating' or 'celebrating' human experience might be better for a beginning, to indicate the pre-occupied passivity before life in which the imagination often starts its work. And 'exploring' can sound too much like wandering for its own sake, as though literature simply opens up successive territories of human response. 'Searching' or even 'ordering' would be better, so long as we didn't imply by either of them an 'irritable reaching after fact and reason'. Every writer – not necessarily in an obvious sense nor necessarily consciously, and whether in a tragic or comic or in any other manner – means what he says. Sometimes he will deny that there is a meaning. 'I only wanted to write an interesting tale,' he will say, ignoring that the interest of a story almost always comes from seeing the human will in action – against chaos or against order. Sometimes the meaning he intends will not be the work's achieved meaning. The ebb and flow of imaginative power within the work may reveal attitudes hidden from the writer himself. But there will be a meaning, a kind of order – expressed or implied. Whether he knows it or not, the writer will be testing the validity of certain ways of seeing life;

* Reprinted here from the version in *About Literature*, Vol. Two of *Speaking To Each Other*, by permission of the author and his publisher, Chatto and Windus.

he will be offering, no matter how provisionally, a way of ordering the flux of experience. By his choice and arrangement of materials, by the temper of his treatment of them, a writer is implicitly saying: this is one way in which we can face experience or succumb to it or seek to alter it or try to ignore it.

The attention good literature pays to life is both loving and detached. It frames experience and, in a sense, distances it. But it always assumes the importance, the worthwhileness, of human experience even when – as in tragedy – it finds much in that experience evil. So, if a writer is imaginatively gifted, his work helps to define and assert that importance, to bring experience up fresh before us. This is not a way of saying that a good writer makes an evil experience good. But his exploration is good, since it defines more clearly the nature of the evil we suffer and perform. It helps to make us believe more in the freely willing nature of man; and it helps us to feel more sharply the difficulties and limits of that freedom. Good literature insists on 'the mass and majesty' of the world – on its concreteness and sensuous reality, and on its meanings beyond 'thisness'. It insists on the importance of the inner, the distinctive and individual, life of man, while much else in our activities and in our make-up – fear, ambition, fatigue, laziness – tries to make that life generalized and typecast.

Not all writing acts in this way. Roughly, we can say there are two kinds of literature: conventional literature and live literature. Conventional literature usually (though it may sometimes do better than its author knows) reinforces existing assumptions, accepted ways of looking at the world. Properly read, live literature – even the quietest or most light-hearted – may be disturbing, may subvert our view of life.

'Properly read' is the key-phrase in that last sentence. I said at the beginning that literature explores, re-creates and orders human experience in a *unique* way. Other activities of the human mind explore human experience, and some re-create it, and some seek to order it. One can think of philosophers or theologians or of composers or painters. I am not concerned to set literature against any of those. Literature can be discursive in the way that some philosophy is; it has, like painting and music but unlike most philosophy, an imaginative architecture. Its peculiarity is its special relationship with, its special form of engagement with, language . . . a relationship which is intellectual and emotional at the same time and is almost always a relationship by values. Ruskin said, 'Tell me what you like and I'll tell you what you are.' We could just as easily say, 'Tell me what language you use and I will tell you what you are.' Language is not simply a range of conventional signs, increasing and altering so as to express the complexity of experience; the business of grappling with the complexity of experience, with the life by time and the life by values, is itself partly carried on through and within language.

Literature can never be aesthetically pure or abstractly contemplative. There can be no such thing as 'abstract literature' as there is abstract painting. By its nature – because its medium, language, is used by almost everybody in all sorts of everyday situations; and because it tries both to say and to be – literature is an art which invites impurities.

It is the most creaturely of the arts. No other art makes us feel so much that the experience must have been just like that, that desire and will and thought would all have been caught up with those gestures, those smells, those sounds. It's not reality; it's a mirroring; but it mirrors more nearly than any other imaginative activity the *whole* sense of an experience.

Literature is both in time and outside time. It is in time because it works best when it creates a sense of a certain time and place and of particular persons, when it works through and re-creates identifiable life and manners ... Tom Jones hiding in a particular copse with Molly Seagrim, Marvell lying in a certain garden, Dimitri Karamazov in *that* prison cell, Will and Anna Brangwen in *that* cottage bedroom.

It is outside time in two ways. First, in a sense we are all used to: that, if it is rooted in time and place and is imaginatively penetrating, it will go beyond particular time and place and speak about our common humanity, will become – as we used to say more readily – universal.

Literature goes beyond time in a more subtle sense. To describe discursively, fully to paraphrase, all that an imaginatively successful scene in fiction or drama or a poem says, means and is – to do this would take an impossibly long time and would be futile. It is of the essence of the scene's or the poem's meaning that all its elements simultaneously co-exist, do their work at the same time ... so that we feel them all at once as we would in heightened moments of life, if we were sufficiently sensitive. The resources of language and form then work together to produce the peculiarly literary achievement, full of simultaneous meanings ... Yeats writing 'the salmon-falls, the mackerel-crowded seas', Cordelia replying 'No cause, no cause', Margaret Wilcox crying, 'Not any more of this! You shall see the connection if it kills you, Henry!', Sophia looking down on Gerald Scales' body after all those years of desertion. One could not, even at six-volume length, 'write out the meaning' of any one of these; in separating the elements by space and time we would destroy the meaning.

To respond to these meanings is not necessarily easy. It is not sensible to expect a work of any depth to yield all its meanings on a first reading by almost anyone in almost any mood. Literature is 'for delight', it is true – delight in recognition, in exploration and in ordering, in the sense of increased apprehension, of new and unsuspected relationships, and in aesthetic achievement. But beyond a fairly simple level (for example, rhythmic incantation) we have to work more and attend better if we want the best rewards, here as in any other activity.

It follows that wide hospitality is good. Nor need it be the enemy of good judgement. The fact that some people use their claim to being hospitable as an excuse for refusing to make distinctions is another matter; catholicity is not promiscuity. Almost every writer with imaginative ability (that is, with some capacity, no matter how intermittent or partial, to explore aspects of experience through language), almost every such writer will have some insights to give if we read him disinterestedly, with a 'willing suspension of disbelief'.

Such a man may in general, or in particular things, be immature or irresponsible; we may think his statements or assumptions about human life untrue or perverse. If we do feel any of these things we should say so, as exactly and strongly as we think necessary. But we ought to be clear what we are attacking. Otherwise we may dismiss a man with some imaginative ability, but whose outlook we find antipathetic, and will claim we are judging his literary powers; or we may come to believe that we find imaginative insight in a writer whose views fit our own but who is without creative ability. If we do not 'entertain as a possibility' the outlook of a writer while we are reading him we shall not know what his outlook is, and will attack or praise a caricature of it.

'To entertain as a possibility' is not the best form of words but it is hard to find a better. It does not mean 'to accept', because the process is more subtle than that. It means to exercise intellectual and emotional openness and charity. It means to be able to see for a while how someone can have such an outlook and to know what it feels like to have it, what the world looks like from that angle. To do this is not to 'surrender'. All the time, though not necessarily consciously, we are testing that outlook against life as we think we know it ourselves. With certain writers we will be all the time in a sharp double state . . . of entertaining and rejecting at once; but even then there are likely to be moments when light is thrown on a part of human experience, and some attitude which we had pushed out of the field of our consciousness will prove to have more power than we had wanted to think.

In my experience, this is likely to be true of all but two kinds of literary effort. It is not true of work which, though full of 'right instincts' and intelligent technicalities, shows no effective literary imagination. Think, for example, of many of the thematic novels about moral conflict published during the past twenty years.

Worse, is the bodilessly aesthetic production which tries to treat words and forms as ends in themselves. I believe that literature is certainly in one sense 'play' – grave and absorbed play. But these are pointless arabesques. They do not explore, and their patterns neither mean nor mirror.

I do not think a trivial outlook will produce great literature. It may produce odd incidental insights; but, overall, a shallow view of life will produce a shallow penetration into experience. But I agree also with R. P. Blackmur who noted that we could learn something from second- and third-rate work, so long as we supplied our own irony towards it. You salt it yourself.

The *effects* of literature cannot be simply described – the moral effects, that is. I do not think these effects are direct, or our experience would be a simpler matter than it is. Good readers might then be good people, and good writers better human beings even than their good readers. In speaking about the moral impact of art we are not talking about a more complicated form of those ethically improving tales for children, most of which are irrelevant to the way imaginative literature actually works. Obviously, we can learn morally even if evil appears to triumph. 'Moral impact' does not mean a direct ethical prompting but the effect literature may have on the temper with which we face experience.

But first, and as we have seen, literature does seek to articulate something of the 'mass and majesty' of experience. Most of us (and most of our societies) are constantly tending to narrow our focus, to ignore embarrassing qualifications and complexities, to make much of the rest of the world and all experience with which we are not comfortable – to make all this into merely a backcloth to the stage on which our egos do act comfortably. Literature can help to bring us up short, to stop the moulds from setting firm. It habitually seeks to break the two-dimensional frame of fixed 'being' which we just as habitually try to put round others, to make us see them again as three-dimensional people in a constant state of 'becoming'. Literature can have only a formal use for utterly damned souls – or for saints.

It is all the time implicitly inviting us to remain responsive and alert and to extend our humanity; we do not talk quite so easily about 'all farm labourers' or even about 'all Russians' after we have read Hardy or Turgenev. It is implicitly inviting us to widen and deepen our knowledge of ourselves and of our relations with others, to realize that life is more this – and more that – than we had been willing to think (Emma at Box Hill, Queequeg looking down into the whale-nursery).

All this, we have to remember, may be achieved – may sometimes only be achieved – in a mythic and parabolic way. When we speak of the 'moral intelligence of art' we are not speaking only of the will in action but also of a world outside the will, of the unconscious psychic life of men. It is almost impossible not to sound pretentious here; but literature – along with the other arts, which have their own ways of informing the imagination – can help us to rediscover awe.

What is true of individuals is true also of societies. A society without a literature has that much less chance of embodying within its temper and so within its organizations something of the fullness of human experience. We only know certain things by articulating them or bodying them out. This does not mean that we have to 'argue them out'. We may know some things only by approaching them metaphorically, as dramatic 'play'.

So literature can make us sense more adequately the fullness, the weight, the inter-relations and the demands of human experience – and the possibilities for order. It can make us feel all this, but not necessarily act on it. We can see and do otherwise, always. But we are not then acting quite so much out of blindness or inarticulateness; we are selfishly or fearfully or wilfully trying to short-circuit what we know underneath to be more nearly the true state of things. Works of literature, properly read, give us the opportunity to extend our imaginative grasp of human experience; if we *will* to act well thereafter we may be able to do so with greater flexibility and insight. In this special sense literature can be morally educative. It can guide the moral will in so far as its illuminations depreciate certain modes of conduct and, conversely, reinforce others. But it cannot direct the moral will. In so far as it embodies moral intelligence and psychic insight it may *inform* the moral will, be 'the soul of all (our) moral being'.

The relation of literature to 'the moral will' is not simple. Literature is 'a criticism of life' which must itself be judged. But we can only understand that criticism and make our own judgement on it if we first – in a sense – suspend the will, if we attend to the literature as itself, as if it were an autonomous object, and let it work in its own way. It may then be in an active relationship with our sense of ourselves, with our sense of life in time and life by values. Like the other arts, literature is involved with ends beyond itself. Things can never be quite the same again after we have read – really read – a good book.

APPENDIX TWO

Relating to various comments made throughout the text

THE APPRECIATION OF LITERATURE
by Lord David Cecil*

Up to a year or two ago, I was for forty years a don at Oxford. It was an agreeable life. Day after day I would sit in my room in college, teaching young people to enjoy themselves. All dons don't do this – historians needn't, or philosophers. But I taught English literature, and that is different. There are many books published in the world and of many kinds, but one category stands apart: books that come under the heading of literature. This means books not written for any ulterior purpose but simply to give the reader a satisfying experience, such as he would have from a piece of music or a beautiful picture: their aim is to delight. Of course, the greatest art does much more. Shakespeare, Tolstoy, Wordsworth, Dante give us wisdom and spiritual vision. But delight is the means. Unless we enjoy their writings, we shall not perceive the vision and the wisdom. Therefore it follows that the first aim of a reader is to be delighted. To do this fully he must develop his faculty of appreciation. That is what I tried to help the young people to do, in my room at Oxford. Appreciation is not a simple process: a lot of professional critics have never learnt how to do it. They seem to take a positive pleasure in telling you that they do not enjoy things. They explain that they think Dickens much overrated, or that they can't stand Charles Lamb – as if not to enjoy what has pleased Tolstoy and Virginia Woolf was something to be proud of. As a matter of fact, to achieve a wide appreciation does need self-training.

First of all, it needs the right approach: one must realize what a work of literary art is; and in particular that it is the result of two impulses. For one thing, it is the record of a personal vision. For example, on a May evening in 1819, Keats sat in a garden in Hampstead and listened to the song of a nightingale. He listened with rapture, and all the more because it was a poignant moment in his life. He had lately been watching his brother, of whom he was very fond, die of consumption. Keats contrasted the grim facts of reality, as he had just seen them, with the sense of bliss

* Reprinted by permission from *The Listener* for 9 December 1971, pp. 797.

stirred in him by the song of the nightingale. A flood of feeling welled up in him – about life and death and beauty and suffering and transitoriness and the yearning of his unsatisfied soul for a happiness not to be found on earth – which poured out in 'Ode to a Nightingale'. Keats wanted to tell us about his feelings. But this was not the only motive for his writing the poem. People don't become painters just because there is one particular subject they want to paint: they also enjoy constructing a pleasing object in line and colour. It is the same with poets. If Keats had just wanted to say what he felt, he could have done it in prose. But he wanted to construct a pleasing object in word and rhythmic verse. It is the blend of the two impulses, the impulse to record the personal vision and the impulse to construct an object in verse, which produced the unique phenomenon called 'Ode to a Nightingale'.

The aim of the reader is to perceive such phenomena and respond to them. This does mean accepting, for the time being, the kind of vision and the kind of form. I stress this again because people often reject one or the other or both. I've heard people say they did not admire Thomas Hardy's novels because they were gloomy. They cannot be forced to like them: but it's no good blaming them for being gloomy. Hardy had a tragic vision of life and that indeed is what the novels portray. People should never start with strong preconceived ideas about what the work ought to be like. Any writer, if he is any good, has something of his own to say. That is his vision; and the new vision nearly always means a slight modification of form. We should try to accept both.

We must also be sure that we understand the language in which the work is composed. I don't mean just the words: but language as a metaphor for its whole mode of expression. Three things are entailed here.

First, there is the convention in which it is written. All literature is written in some convention; and failure to realize this has led very clever people to say very foolish things. Voltaire was one of the cleverest men who ever lived, but he had been brought up on the French classical tragedy of Racine and Corneille: formal, restrained, regular. That was his idea of tragedy. He came to England and went to see *Hamlet*. He thought it appalling: a crude barbaric mixture of verse and prose, poetry and realism, crammed with ghosts, corpses, maniacs – all very unlike Racine. But we must not be too scornful of foreign Voltaire. A little later Hazlitt, one of our best critics, but who was brought up on Shakespeare, read Racine. He didn't react quite as strongly as Voltaire, but he thought it poor stuff: artificial, pedantic, dull. He hadn't accepted its convention. As a matter of fact, Shakespeare and Racine were both great writers and also not as unlike as all that: they were both masters of passionate, noble tragedy, but expressed in different conventions, both of which the reader should learn to accept.

I once failed to do this myself with disastrous results. When I was twenty-one I went to see my first Chekhov play – *The Cherry Orchard*, it may have been. I thought the way the characters talked unreal. People didn't seem to reply to each other. One might say, 'How noisy the birds are,' and another would reply: 'I've not had a good education, though it was in Moscow.' Also they were strangely outspoken, and might say to each other: 'Why do you bore me so much?' I thought it all very unreal. I was not used to the convention by which Chekhov, in order to reveal what was in the minds of his characters, would make them utter it straight out. If they were thinking about being educated in Moscow, they said so; and if they were bored, they told each other so. Of course, it may have been that in Chekhov's world people did talk like this. But they don't do so in other Russian books. I think it is his convention. In fact, as he had extraordinary insight into human nature, this convention makes him convey the reality of the independent lives and thoughts of his different people about what is happening to them much better than he could have without it. Now I say categorically that the most realistic plays I've ever read or seen are the plays of Chekhov.

The second language to be learnt is the language of period. This applies less to modern than to older works. A past period is like a foreign country. It is a region inhabited by human beings of like passions to our own, but with different customs and traditions. If we don't understand these customs and traditions we shall misunderstand books of that particular period. Let me take an instance from Shakespeare's *Measure for Measure*. In this play Isabella, the heroine, refuses Angelo's dishonourable proposal to her though it would save Claudio her brother's life if she yielded; and she does this in spite of the fact that Claudio beseeches her to yield. For her refusal, Isabella has received a great deal of blame from subsequent critics, who call her a hard-hearted prude. In fact, to blame her is to show a fatal ignorance of the beliefs of Shakespeare's age, according to which if she had agreed, she would have committed a mortal sin and been in danger of hell. And Claudio would have been too, for urging her to yield. She cannot therefore be blamed much for refusing.

Finally, one must learn what I would call the language of the author's personality and temperament. This is a more complex task. Every book is the expression of a man or a woman and to approach the book properly one must adapt oneself to his viewpoint. Each author has his private window on reality, different from other men's windows. Different things are visible from it, and the same things are seen in a different proportion and different perspective. One must try, while reading, to look at every book from that author's particular window and see life from his viewpoint. Now this third language is much the hardest to learn, for each of us has his own viewpoint and can't divest himself of it entirely. It is hard for a militant atheist to appreciate a religious book, for a puritan type to like Tom Jones. This is a particular difficulty in judging contemporary work. Hazlitt said, very truly, that all living authors are our friends or our foes. I remember, when I was young, that progressive pacific kinds of people could not admire Kipling because he represented the militant imperialism which they disliked. At the same time, militant imperialist kinds of people couldn't admire Shaw, who, they thought, was a dangerous socialist revolutionary. Both were wrong: Kipling and Shaw are both writers of genius. Now it is easy to realize this because they no longer stand for living controversies: Kipling's brand of imperialism and Shaw's brand of revolutionary socialism are both things of the past. What remains is their genius; and we respond to that freely.

Of course, human imperfection will always limit our powers of appreciation. I've never been able fully to enjoy what I am told is the best novel written in my lifetime: James Joyce's *Ulysses*. I recognize Joyce's genius, and that there are bright flashes of it in *Ulysses*. But, in the main, I find it often boring and sometimes repellent. But I also realize that this is partly because it is so far from my individual taste in subject and style that I have not been able to learn its language. On the other hand, Jane Austen's view of life and type of art are so naturally sympathetic to me that it is possible – though I don't think it is probable – that I overrate her. Yet the fact that one will never be perfectly good is no reason for not trying to be as good as one can be; and, in the same way, the fact that one will never achieve a perfectly just and comprehensive taste is no reason for not trying to refine and broaden one's taste as much as one can. Certainly, now I am sixty-eight years old I do enjoy a lot of books that I didn't enjoy at eighteen. Then I had a romantic taste in poetry; I thought it ought to be dreamy and rapturous and inspiring; and I found it extraordinary when somebody said to me that he liked Pope's poetry as much as Keats's. Now I delight in Pope; but I still like Keats as much as ever. Nor does this broadening of taste make it undiscriminating. On the contrary, it grows more impartial but also more discriminating: because, having adapted the mind to the convention, to the period, to the personality, one is much more able to take the work on its own terms and thus perceive more clearly when it fails. One gets less partisan, one is able to see faults even in one's favourites. I delight in Jane Austen, largely because I think her stories so true to life. But for this very reason I notice all the

more when I think they are not. I find the end of *Mansfield Park*
unconvincing. There, if you remember, Henry Crawford, having
been refused by the heroine Fanny, goes off and elopes with an
old flame, Mrs Rushworth. For me the reason for this is clear:
Jane Austen wants to get him out of the way so that Fanny can
marry the hero Edmund. Also she wants to emphasize that Henry
really was a very undesirable type. All the same, I think the incident improbable because he has been represented up till then as a
cold, careful character. Why then should he involve himself with a
woman he was already tired of? It is not made clear. Perhaps
Jane Austen was aware of this, for having stated the fact of the
elopement briefly, she says airily: 'Let other pens dwell on guilt
and misery, I quit such odious subjects as soon as I can.' One
may sympathize with her in this. All the same, she was mistaken.
She needed to dwell a little on the 'odious subject' if she was to
make her story convincing.

To develop appreciation means that one notes faults as well as
merits. Yet the gain in pleasure is greater than the loss. For to
train one's taste is to increase one's capacity for enjoyment: it
enables one to enter into such a variety of experience. That is
the great gift literature can give one. In real life, experience is
limited. The same person cannot be both a man and a woman, a
saint and a sinner, a stay-at-home and an explorer, an ancient
Roman and a modern Russian. But books can teach us all to be
all those things in imagination. The Lady of Shalott sat in her
tower watching the diverse pageant of human life pass before her
in a mirror. The reader is like her: he sits watching the diverse
pageant of human thought and human feeling passing across the
gleaming mirror of literature. And like the Lady of Shalott's, it is
a magic mirror, for it turns all it reflects into matter for delight.
It is not so in reality. Reality is often very much lacking in delight.
So is the reality described in books. Let me mention three favourites: *War and Peace*, *The Mayor of Casterbridge* by Thomas Hardy
and *Emma*. None of them represents life at its most attractive.
The battles in *War and Peace* are the last things I would like to be
present at. It would be sad to live in Hardy's Casterbridge. Emma's
home is pleasanter; but it is a little dull. Yet I enjoy reading about
all three. In them, by the magic power of art, lead and mud have
been turned into gold; horror, gloom, dullness, because they have
been made part of the vision of a great writer and transfigured by
his art, are changed into matter for delight. And it is a delight
that lasts. I am now an elderly retired person, and as such I look
back over the years and ask myself what satisfactions have proved
the most lasting. Many have not lasted. I am too old any longer
to play games or dance; my social life is restricted; and I cannot,
as I used, take much interest in the future of the world, for I

shan't live long enough to see what is going to happen in it. But
the satisfaction given by reading is unimpaired. Prose and poetry,
novels and plays, essays and biographies – I enjoy them all as
much as ever. The world round me may have grown dimmer with
the passing of the years, but not the world reflected in the magic
mirror of literature. That is still as fresh and vivid and fascinating
and enthralling as it was when I was fifteen years old.

APPENDIX THREE

Relating to Chapter Six

TALKING ABOUT BOOKS
by Andrew Stibbs*

Teachers too often treat a book's qualities as gems locked behind combinations which teachers know by culture's code. By our standards, but not necessarily theirs, adolescents' tastes are eclectic: Ballantyne, Beano, Barstow, Blyton, Brontë, Bond. That is not surprising. Their needs, sensibilities and educations are not ours, and their shopping list of values (excitement, immediacy, and relevance) is not a teacher's. You can sort junk with a magnet or a sieve. Neither isolates gems. And what is left in the sieve is still junk to the magnet.

Why should adolescents' tastes in books differ so much from ours? That fiction, like adolescence, is in an unprecedented situation, has always been true, but is more so now. New media compete with print and condition us to techniques different from those traditional to fiction. The typical television fiction is short (the episode); the typical story long (the novel). Good programmes start quickly; good novels slowly. Postponing pleasure is not fashionable. Paperbacks and new uses of leisure ensure that no classic is read as the only entertainment available. Our pupils were born into an electronic age. They value immediacy more than us.

H: 'If it hasn't got an interesting cover I don't bother with it.'

They are more different from us than we were from our teachers. Where teachers talk about books in terms of character, language, symbolism, genre, pupils assess them as stories, even if, in essays, they humour us by dutifully regurgitating examinese. That is why they value an intriguing title. 'Recently I read *Bang Your Dead* by Henry Treece. I liked this because it had an exciting title, a good front cover and the story was not slow and boring.' They like 'a story which does not spend too long explaining and describing things'.

A book the girls pass round is *To Sir With Love*.

* Reprinted by permission from *The Times Educational Supplement* for 7 July 1972, p. 40.

J: '. . . I think us girls liked it because . . . we go to school and we've never had any coloured teachers . . .'

They engage with fiction by identifying. They regard the story as an extension of experience ('. . . we've never had . . .'), but as a possibility for them ('. . . we go to school . . .').

G: 'The fiction books I like most are the more up-to-date to life ones . . . about children themselves – you've got to put yourself in that situation – it helps you a lot really.'

Because they seek personal experience in books they are scornful of most 'children's fiction' which they say is about Romans and 'teenagers in the fifties'. They can generalize about vicarious experience if it is contemporary.

H (on a novel about schools): 'It's made me more in favour of comprehensive schools.'

There is no escapism in their attitudes. To an adult there seems a too limiting commitment to the contemporary: when I recommend *Huckleberry Finn* as a better novel on the colour problem than *To Sir With Love*, they say 'but the colour problem's not like that now'. They are right.

The quality of a collection depends on the quantity of junk it is collected from. A teacher's responsibility is to provide a lot of material, not to determine taste. A large collection of paperbacks in the English room should encourage more, quicker, and more interested reading, and (since the books will be passed round) group discussion.

The girls in the conversation pass books round among themselves like boys do with sex 'n' violence paperbacks. Then they talk about them, most commonly in phrases like '. . . that bit where she . . .', 'oo yes, and when he . . .' – a confirmatory sharing, a communal reaction (talk) to a personal activity (reading). It is an attempt to relate their own experience, real and vicarious, to that of other people, and relationships are easiest made over shortest distances. To encourage such communality may be a remaining justification for the institution of the school, whose purpose I take to be to maximize contact with a variety of things, ideas, and other people.

In classroom discussion they all talk at once (instead of saying nothing), they go off 'the subject' (on to something more interesting), they make 'wrong' interpretations (according to what the teacher learnt), and they talk in terms of 'if it had been me . . .' (instead of character, language, symbolism, genre). J wrote: 'It is best to have a discussion because then you use your own opinion, but if you write about it you use other people's ideas and then you don't really write about your views'. It is by conversation that we communicate with others, share ideas, and order most of our experience. Conversation is more mind-changing, more educative, than writing.

The 'teacher' can ensure conversation by ritualizing it, power it by casual questions, and provide raw material – enriched literary junk. (Books discussed in the recorded conversation included *Fahrenheit 451* and *My Oedipus Complex.*) Providing books is one thing. Recommending them directly is another, maybe counterproductive, thing. 'When books are recommended by your own age group you tend to go for those rather than the ones a teacher would recommend.'

G: '. . . you have it really in the back of your mind all the time oh I'm being forced to read this book . . . so I don't really enjoy reading them.'

In spite of the exclusive contemporaneity they claim for their tastes ('up-to-date to life'), this group referred, favourably, to Brontë, Ballantyne, and Blyton. They have had a lot of junk to go at, and they have sorted some strange collections from it. The best use of junk is not for its original purpose.

The quotations are from a group of unselected fourth-year secondary pupils. The initialled ones are taken from a conversation recorded for BBC Radio Teesside's programme 'For Young Readers'.

APPENDIX FOUR

Relating to Chapter Eight

PENGUIN'S NEST AND AFTER*

by DAVID STEWART (*Director, Charles Wilson (Booksellers) Ltd., Liverpool*) and PETER KENNERLEY (*I. M. Marsh College of Education*)

Some six years ago Peter Kennerley found a problem in a large Boys' Grammar School where the teaching of English was hindered by the inability of the boys to obtain books other than library books. This was due partly to the general apathy about buying books, but mainly to the distance of the school from the nearest bookshops. To remedy this a school bookshop was suggested. Nobody at that time had very much idea about how this would work, or even if it would work at all, but we were prepared to take a chance and see what happened.

The school had available a small ex-biology lab, situated at the top of three flights of stairs in an old building – just about as far from the centres of school life as possible. At first sight this seemed to be a most unsuitable site for a bookshop, but it proved to be very successful because it was a place that people liked to visit, a social centre, well away from other activities and possibly from the presence of the staff.

Considerable advance publicity was given. With the aid of the school's art department Penguins, Puffins and Pelicans galore were produced and every available space all over the school was covered with posters announcing the imminent opening of the 'Penguin's Nest'. The name was apt and attracted a great deal of attention both within the school and outside and after three weeks of this intensive publicity opening day arrived to a complete sell-out of all available space, and most of the available stock. The response was tremendous; the stock had been a very wide choice covering all ages from 11+ to the 6th Form and repeat orders had to be supplied within a day or two of the opening. The shop was open every lunch hour and occasionally after school. Senior pupils were recruited to help; orders were taken for titles not in stock and all departments were asked for their suggestions. As

* Reprinted by permission from *Bookselling News*, Vol. 6 No. 12, December 1970.

nearly as possible normal shop routine was followed and from then until the end of term frequent injections of fresh stock kept up the momentum while titles in which no interest had been shown were replaced.

At the end of term we took stock and checked the accounts. We found to our slightly astonished delight that over £150 worth of paperbacks had been sold in a little over 8 weeks. At a rate of about 6 paperbacks to the £1 at that time, this meant that a total of 900 books had been sold to 800 boys where previously virtually no books at all had been bought. This was obviously a very successful venture indeed, and has continued to be ever since, despite various interruptions through changes of staff and building demolition which has destroyed the old Penguin's Nest. It has met with almost universal approval – including that of the H.M. Inspectors who browsed and bought for themselves when they visited the school. It has now become so much a part of school life that a new and permanent home has been found and fitted out by the County Education authority.

As this had been so successful we tried circularizing local schools. This was not very rewarding but at least one or two showed interest and amongst these were a Teacher Training College and a Technical College, both of which were a long way from any other book outlets. Gradually, word of the scheme spread among local teachers with very little help from us. Within two years 30 such agencies were started covering every single type of school: Colleges of Education and Further Education, Comprehensive Schools, Grammar and Secondary Modern schools, state and Church Primary schools and even private schools. All have one thing in common – enthusiasm for the scheme.

All but a very few have been successful in varying degrees. Most of them are run by a member of staff but some by senior pupils. The accounting has been kept to a minimum and although there are now 52 agencies there has been no problem with procedures; no loss of stock through damage and virtually none through 'shop-lifting'. It takes about 2–3 hours of David Stewart's time each week to run the scheme with longer periods at the end of term when visits are made to most of the schools. The children's paperback stock has been enlarged to carry nearly every available title and this stock is constantly interchanged between schools and the shop; very little is left unsold at each school at the end of term. Each agency is made as economic as possible with a stock turn of 3–4 times a year. Occasionally most of them augment their stock and give special displays for Parents' Nights and Open Days and these are always most successful. A number of schools have asked first for an exhibition and then followed on with a permanent book agency.

One of the most exciting and rewarding features of running such schemes is the constant and regular contact which this gives us with each school. The bookseller feels he has a branch in each and is drawn into a great deal of school activity, all of which is of great benefit. The cash profit obviously varies considerably between each school. The average turnover is about £30 a term with some as high as £100 and the schools receive the usual agency discount of 10 per cent on what they sell. In many cases the schools spend this on library books.

However wide his interests and altruistic his motives, the bookseller has to be concerned with his profit and these schemes have proved profitable. The teacher running the agency takes no financial risk and can concentrate on making his 'shop' a cultural centre in which many children to whom books are alien objects can be drawn gradually to know the delight which they hold. The school agency may also be of incalculable value to the teachers if it helps to keep them in contact with fresh ideas and approaches.

There are a number of basic rules founded on our original experience with the Penguin's Nest, but 6 years and over 50 agencies later we have found very little which needed changing. To be successful the school must be enthusiastic. Booksellers must not over-sell the idea to a school because its success depends entirely on an enthusiastic member or members of staff willing to devote considerable time and effort to the scheme. The only failures were where a school was persuaded to try the idea but lacked this vital enthusiasm. The bookseller too must be just as enthusiastic and willing to spend time and trouble visiting the school to see that everything is working as it should. After the first term the school will know what has to be done and visits can be cut to about two a term.

The bookseller must also of course provide the stock and be prepared to badger paperback publishers into providing stands and publicity material. They have been very cooperative in this, particularly Penguin and Pan. Finally, the bookseller must be able to see beyond the immediate cash profit to the long term benefits.

These are for the bookseller the creation of a very large book-buying public in the schools. In these 52 agencies there must be something approaching 25,000 schoolchildren growing up with a bookshop in their midst aware for the first time in their lives that books can be bought and owned and are cheap, instead of the awful and eternal cry that 'books are free' and only to be borrowed, begged or stolen. If more such agencies were organized over the country by enthusiastic booksellers the benefits to the trade would be quite startling.

Index